The Future of War

The Future of War

Organizations as Weapons

MARK D. MANDELES

Potomac Books, Inc.
Washington, D.C.

Library of Congress Cataloging-in-Publication Data

Mandeles, Mark David, 1950–
    The future of war : organizational structures for the revolution in
  military affairs / Mark D. Mandeles. — 1st ed.
      p. cm.
    Includes bibliographical references and index.
    ISBN 1-57488-630-4 (hardcover : alk. paper) — ISBN 1-57488-631-2
  (pbk. : alk. paper)   1. United States Armed Forces—Organization.
  2. United States. Dept. of Defense—Organization.   3. Military art
  and science—Technological innovations.   4. Organizational behavior.
  I. Title.
  UA23.M2785   2005
  355.3'0973—dc22   2005009941

ISBN 1-57488-630-4
ISBN 1-57488-631-2

(alk. paper)

Printed in Canada on acid-free paper that meets the American National Standards Institute Z39-48 Standard.

Potomac Books, Inc.
22841 Quicksilver Drive
Dulles, Virginia 20166

First Edition

10 9 8 7 6 5 4 3 2 1

This book is dedicated to

Chad, Yuriko, and Masayo Mandeles

Jay and Alice Meisel, and Meredith, Sam, and Emma Meisel

Gerald J. Lederman

Bruce Adler

Lewis and Ann Dolinsky

Harriet and Lee Philips, Lenore Philips, and Matthew, Laura, Sally, and Joshua Philips

Contents

List of Acronyms

ABCCC Airborne Battlefield Command and Control Center
ATO air tasking order
AWACS Airborne Warning and Control System
BDA battle damage assessment
C^2 command and control
C^3I command, control, communications, and intelligence
C^4I command, control, communication, computer, and intelligence
C^4ISR command, control, communication, computer, intelligence, surveillance, and reconnaissance
GAT guidance, apportionment, and targeting
JFACC Joint Force Air Component Commander
JSTARS Joint Surveillance Attack Radar System
NATO North Atlantic Treaty Organization
OODA observe, orient, decide, act
RMA revolution in military affairs
ROE rules of engagement
SAC strategic air command
SHAPE Supreme Headquarters Allied Powers Europe
SOP standard operation procedure
SPINS special instructions

Acknowledgments

I have received helpful critical written and oral comments from knowledgeable, kind, and gracious colleagues in writing this book, including Col. David A. Anhalt (USAF, ret.), Dr. David André (Colonel, USA, ret.), Dr. Thomas C. Hone, Capt. George Kasten (USN), Dr. Todd R. LaPorte, Dr. Martin Landau, Col. Marc Lindsley (USAF, ret.), Dr. Karley Little, Dr. Frank Mahncke, Laura L. Mandeles, Andrew W. Marshall, Jacob Neufeld, C. Edward Peartree, Brig. Gen. Paul Selva (USAF), Nathan P. Shockey, Lt. Gen. Philip D. Shutler (USMC, ret.), Dr. Jacob A. Stockfisch, Truman R. Strobridge, and Capt. Jan M. van Tol (USN). The interlibrary loan staff of the Fairfax County Public Library system chased down many otherwise unavailable publications. In addition, I received kind and professional administrative assistance from the staff of the Office of Net Assessment; in particular, Rebecca C. Bash and M. Sgt. J. J. Mincy-Baker (USAF) resolved innumerable problems with good humor and panache. Last, but not least, Fritz Heinzen provided indispensable advice, support, and help, as did the Potomac Books editors, Rick Russell and Jehanne Moharram, as well as Michie Shaw, Julie Kimmel, and Lisa Camner in the production phase.

I alone am responsible for any substantive or conceptual errors they were unsuccessful in persuading me to remove.

CHAPTER 1

Introduction

We can . . . never know or understand all the implications of any theory, or its full significance.[1]

Over the last few years, many military observers and analysts have pronounced that the U.S. military is undergoing a revolution in military affairs (RMA), a qualitative improvement in operational concepts and weapons that will lead to a transformation in the nature and character of warfare. So many have discussed the RMA that a mere accounting of their work would amount to a major bibliographic essay. Most commentators focus on military technology and argue that new sensor, surveillance, communications, and computational technologies will usher in a period in which the United States will have military capabilities far in excess of potential competitors.[2] In June 1999 renowned military historian John Keegan announced in London's *Daily Telegraph* that the principal components of an information-based military revolution—new munitions and weapons, new reconnaissance and surveillance equipment, new targeting techniques, and smaller and faster

[1]Karl R. Popper, *Unended Quest: An Intellectual Autobiography* (LaSalle, IL: Open Court Publishing, 1976), 28.

[2]For example see Henry C. Bartlett, G. Paul Holman Jr., and Timothy E. Somes, "Force Planning, Military Revolutions and the Tyranny of Technology," *Strategic Review* (Fall 1996): 28–40; Theodor W. Galdi, "Revolution in Military Affairs? Competing Concepts, Organizational Responses, Outstanding Issues," Congressional Research Service 95-1170F (11 December 1995); Barry R. Schneider and Lawrence E. Grinter, eds., *Battlefield of the Future: 21st Century Warfare Issues* (Maxwell AFB, AL: Air University Press, 1998).

computers—allow aircraft to hit intended targets with consistent regularity and thus redefine military capabilities.

Despite the absence of North Atlantic Treaty Organization (NATO) combat casualties attending the 1999 air campaign in Kosovo, whether the new technologies themselves have the desired military effects or will lead to a change in the character of warfare has not been revealed. A good deal of damage in Kosovo resulted from people—on the ground—fighting with only rifles and sidearms. Some evidence even indicates that Serbian President Slobodan Milosevic capitulated because of his fear of an imminent NATO ground attack.[3] Clearly, new technologies will present a new set of problems to military and civilian leaders and to the people assigned to accomplish military tasks.

Analysis of new military problems that may arise over time should begin with the awareness that competition between democratic and nondemocratic states will continue for many years. This long-term potential for conflict leads to three broad questions for U.S. leaders: How do U.S. leaders want to be able to perform military tasks? How do they want to shape opportunities to employ military force? How can U.S. forces perform their tasks most effectively? Generally, questions such as these invoke responses that concentrate on military technology. For example, during a congressional hearing in late 1998, Dr. Jacques Gansler, the Under Secretary of Defense for Acquisition and Technology, made a passing reference to the "revolution in military affairs." Gansler, discussing the budgets for modernization of military forces, appealed for increased "funding on enhanced and secure C³I [command, control, communications, and intelligence] and long-range all-weather precision weap-

---

[3]Dana Priest, "A Decisive Battle That Never Was," *Washington Post*, 19 September 1999, A1, A30. See also Daniel L. Byman and Matthew C. Waxman, "Kosovo and the Great Air Power Debate," *International Security* 24 (Spring 2000): 7.

ons—implementing the full capability of 'reconnaissance/strike warfare' (the essence of the 'Revolution in Military Affairs')."[4] In this short statement Gansler conflated higher technical performance with greater operational capability—an identity relationship that does not necessarily exist[5]—and neglected the impact of the operational concepts and organizational structures on the conduct of combat.

Discussions about military revolutions too often ignore or only pay lip service to the role of military organization in achieving a qualitative improvement in combat capability. They omit the relationship between organization structure and outcomes; the problems of coordination in large organizations composed of many people and offices having specialized roles; and the problems of calculation, attention, and memory that face individuals making decisions with inadequate or ambiguous information under short deadlines or in stressful situations.

The passage of time inevitably brings social, political, and technological changes to organizations. In historical accounts of change, organizations or activities may become smaller or larger. In addition to fluctuations in the size of military force structures, however, qualitative changes, such as the emergence of distinctly new institutions, new organizational forms, and new technologies (e.g., improvements in resolution of remote

---

[4]Jacques S. Gansler, Under Secretary of Defense (Acquisition and Technology), "Statement," *Hearing on DOD Modernization*, House of Representatives, National Security Committee, Subcommittee on Military Procurement and Subcommittee on Research and Development, 106th Cong., 1st sess., 8 October 1998. See also Jacques S. Gansler, "Powering Up for 2000: Defense Strategy for an Uncertain Future," speech presented to Navy League Sea-Air-Space Exposition, 31 March 1999; Jacques S. Gansler, "Technology 2000: Meeting Defense Needs in an Evolving Geopolitical Environment," speech presented to Tech Trends 2000 Conference, 7 April 1999; Jacques S. Gansler, Statement before Senate Armed Services Committee, Subcommittee on Emerging Threats and Capabilities, 106th Cong., 2d sess., 20 April 1999.

[5]Jacob A. Stockfisch, *Plowshares into Swords: Managing the American Defense Establishment* (New York: Mason and Lipscomb, 1973), 155–156.

sensing equipment), also occur.[6] Identifying such qualitative change is critical in preparing for a potential military revolution. Organization has always been central to the planning and conduct of combat. As Sir Michael Howard noted, of all the military innovations of the nineteenth century, the appearance of a new type of organization—the Prussian General Staff—was the most significant.[7]

A critical source of successful military performance in the twenty-first century will be the institutional-organizational structure of society; for a military organization, the key to future combat effectiveness is not technology but rather this institutional and organizational structure and its effect upon incentives to invent and innovate. Significant challenges for the U.S. military will be organizing engagement in conflict more effectively, eschewing incentives to substitute short-term gains for long-term advantages, and maintaining incentives for effective long-term innovation.

Outline of the Book

Establishing the importance of organizations in combat capability is not the principal purpose of this study, although the role of organizations will be addressed in the context of the RMA. This work's principal focus will be analysis of assumptions implicit in discussions about the RMA—and how we should view the relationship among organizations, operational concepts, and technology. In addition, this research will present, describe, and categorize properties of notional combat or-

---

[6]Richard R. Nelson, "Economic Growth via the Coevolution of Technology and Institutions," in *Evolutionary Economics and Chaos Theory*, eds. Loet Leydesdorff and Peter Van den Besselaar (New York: St. Martin's Press, 1994), 21.

[7]Michael Howard, *War in European History* (Oxford: Oxford University Press, 1976), 100.

ganizational structures, equipped with RMA-type equipment and operational concepts, executing both operational-level and tactical-level operations. Chapters 2 and 3 discuss the methodological and conceptual tools essential to analyzing how the U.S. military may evolve into the mid-twenty-first century. Chapter 4 reviews organization and decision making in the Persian Gulf War's air campaign to illustrate issues the American national security establishment will face in the twenty-first century. Chapter 5 describes "network-centric warfare," an emerging operational concept. Chapter 6 proposes and compares organizational structures that may be used to implement a concept such as network-centric warfare. The final chapter takes stock of what we know—and what we need to know—to build a twenty-first-century RMA force.

It might appear simpler for the reader to begin this analysis of assumptions and of future military organization with chapter 5's discussion of network-centric warfare. However, adequate understanding of chapter 5 and of chapter 6's discussion of future notional organizational structures depends on the methodological context provided by chapter 2, which explores the role of historical analysis in examining alternative futures and in making valid inferences about the future, and by chapter 3, which explains the necessity of viewing warfare from multiple levels of analysis. Chapter 3 also illustrates the power of this approach through description of Bloch's analysis of warfare, a successful RMA study written a century ago. Chapter 4's historical analysis of the Persian Gulf War shows some obstacles that will have to be overcome as we digitize the U.S. military and apply the concepts of network-centric warfare.

CHAPTER 2

History, Inferences, and Learning

Like most of those who study history, he [Napoleon III] learned from the mistakes of the past how to make new ones.[1]

Both the popular press and professional military journals abound with arguments that (1) the dissolution of the former Soviet Union fundamentally altered the national security environment and (2) the U.S. military is undergoing a military revolution wherein a set of technologies, associated operational concepts, and new organizations will transform the nature and character of warfare.

When such major changes occur in the security environment and in military capabilities, existing organizations, programs, and habits no longer work as well as they once did. The national security community now faces a greater variety of increasingly complex situations. Types of conflict range from conventional war against state-organized military forces to terrorist attacks conducted by state-supported or non-state-supported groups. Organizational structures and programs created to respond to the Soviet Union are becoming more vulnerable to failures resulting from actions by remote, uncontrollable, and unpredictable sources. Previously established means-ends relationships between the U.S. force structure and the Soviet threat already have been attenuated in the current global security environment.

---

[1]A. J. P. Taylor, "Mistaken Lessons from the Past," cited in *The Oxford Dictionary of Quotations*, ed. Angela Partington (Oxford: Oxford University Press, 1992), 679.

In some important respects, this situation appears analogous to the security challenges that faced the British government in 1775. Britain's decisive 1763 victory over France in the Seven Years War dramatically changed its security environment. The victory enlarged Britain's North American empire to include Canada, the eastern half of the Mississippi Valley, Florida, and the Gulf Coast West Indies islands. The administration of such vast territories imposed severe financial costs on the British government while creating new opportunities for Britain's adversaries. Government leaders decided to enhance their control of the American colonies by deploying a regular army and recouping part of the expense from colonial revenues. They also tightened some features of colonial administration, such as the application of trade laws. Part of Britain's decision to be "firm" with the colonies stemmed from concern that the French, seeking an opportunity to redress their 1763 defeat, would try to encourage the colonies to defy British rule.

The British government confronted the postwar security environment with world-leading naval technology. It not only led continental rivals in solving the navigational problem of determining longitude but also demonstrated its ability to transport significant military forces to the new world in a timely fashion. Yet, at the same time, British administrative organizations, procedures, and modes of behavior made mounting military operations to deal successfully with colonial challenges more difficult. Governmental administrative organizations proved incapable of effectively discharging tasks as assigned because of patronage, corruption, and simple incompetence. Demonstrated merit alone never led to either appointment or promotion to key military positions. Since ad hominem premises and irrelevant factors so strongly influenced their arguments and debates, the British war planners found it extremely difficult to match national security ends with military means or to evaluate the effectiveness of tactics and operations. Only when forced to confront Napoleon on the Continent, after its unsuccessful war for America, did the British government begin to make administrative reforms that aligned military ends with organizational means.[2]

Across the channel, the French monarchy faced similar problems of patronage, corruption, and incompetence in the management of its military affairs. Napoleon, in sharp contrast to the British leaders, devoted a great deal of attention to military organization and the problems stemming from ineffective administration. He noted that "if France in 1790 managed to raise good armies so promptly, it was only because it had a good foundation which the flight of the aristocrats improved rather than made worse."[3] Without the necessity to make patronage appointments of aristocrats, Napoleon gained the advantage of employing some merit criteria in the appointment and promotion of officers.

The kinds of problems and challenges confronted by the British leaders in 1775—a new security environment, new military capabilities, and inadequate administrative means—also test U.S. leaders today. The current U.S. security community has devoted a great deal of thought and analysis to potential threats in the security environment and to technical capabilities of weapons systems. Yet, too little attention has been paid to the ability of military organizations at the tactical and operational level to create the circumstances that permit new technologies and operational concepts to be employed effectively, except by costly ad hoc trial-and-error in war.

The costs of this inattention could be very high if the United States engages in long-term combat against a dedicated, wily, and competent adversary. Even short encounters with incom-

---

[2]Piers MacKesy, *The War for America, 1775–1783* (Lincoln: University of Nebraska Press, 1993).

[3]Jay Luvaas, ed. and trans., *Napoleon on the Art of War* (New York: Free Press, 1999), 73.

petent foes result in high personnel and material costs. In 1987 two Exocet cruise missiles fired by an Iraqi F-1 Mirage attacked the USS *Stark* (FFG 31) while it was on patrol in Persian Gulf international waters. The ship did not fire at the cruise missiles or aircraft in self-defense. It was struck by both missiles.[4] The United States and Iraq were nominal allies at that time; American warships plied the Persian Gulf waters to protect international shipping from Iranian attacks. No one expected the Iraqis to attack a U.S. Navy ship. This attack raises four critical unanswered questions that relate to the design and performance of military organizations during peacetime: How well will units untested in actual combat perform in the first minutes of battle? How do we know when training has been sufficient? In peacetime, how does one choose and promote officers who will be effective in combat? How well will organizations designed in peacetime perform in combat? Neglecting such questions risks mitigating combat effectiveness. The military must ask itself these questions; otherwise the peacetime political system may impose agenda and decision criteria on the military that militate against serious and deep analysis.[5]

James Q. Wilson argues that militaries are "procedural organizations," defined as organizations in which leaders can observe what their subordinates do (e.g., fly some number of sorties each day) but not the outcome from that effort (e.g., the wartime effects on the enemy). In peacetime, leaders can supervise training, developmental testing of equipment, and deployments. Yet, they cannot test these elements of military

---

[4]See Jeffrey L. Levison and Randy L. Edwards, *Missile Inbound: The Attack on the Stark in the Persian Gulf* (Annapolis, MD: Naval Institute Press, 1997).

[5]Unfortunately, the military has resisted asking such questions in too many cases. There is a large literature examining this issue. See for example Jacob A. Stockfisch, *Plowshares into Swords* (New York: Mason and Lipscomb, 1973); and James G. Burton, *The Pentagon Wars* (Annapolis, MD: Naval Institute Press, 1993).

organization in the only way that matters: in combat.[6] These conditions make a procedural organization susceptible to goal displacement, which occurs when an organization's goals (e.g., victory) cannot be connected operationally with its actions (e.g., training and equipping). As a result, the organization's decisions are judged against subordinate goals (or measures of effectiveness) that are more easily connected with its actions.

Goal displacement does not cultivate military organizations that cannot learn quickly or change; it breeds military organizations that may change or adopt new administrative processes or procedures—some in response to political initiatives or demands—that have little to do with military victory. In the early 1960s the military services learned to adjust to the demands of then-new Secretary of Defense Robert S. McNamara for systems analysis and planning, programming, and budgeting, and they became quite adept at manipulating information forwarded to the Office of the Secretary of Defense (OSD).[7] The services adapted to their political environment, accommodating the decision criteria and systems analysis tools employed by OSD analysts. Yet, when the world changes and new security environments arise, as with the dissolution of the Soviet Union, the effectiveness of military organizations well adapted to their previous political environments is put at risk.

---

[6]James Q. Wilson, *Bureaucracy: What Government Agencies Do and Why They Do It* (New York: Basic Books, 1989), 163. A few limited peacetime tests do illuminate wartime performance. For instance, can a navigator find targets at night? Does tracer machine-gun ammunition provide more information to the shooter or to the intended target? I thank Jacob A. Stockfisch for his insights in a personal communication about testing.

[7]Paul Y. Hammond, "Functional Analysis of Defense Department Decisionmaking in the McNamara Administration," *American Political Science Review* 62, no. 1 (March 1968): 57–69; Stockfisch, *Plowshares into Swords*, 146–147; Jacob A. Stockfisch, "Incentives and Information Quality in Defense Management," R-1827-ARPA (Santa Monica, CA: RAND, August 1976).

Given the large number of Clausewitzian thinkers in the U.S. national security community and the ritualistic injunctions to read *On War*, it is surprising that no one has applied the concept of "friction" to the problem of ameliorating or reducing error deriving from wartime control and coordination of field forces, air forces, and fleets. The concept of error is central to understanding organizations and especially organizational design because the primary objective of a design is to obviate failure. Thus, the starting point for any analysis of military organizations—including private and public civilian organizations—is to remember that they are not fault free: they operate with imperfect information; they program solutions prematurely; they attempt to negotiate uncertainty away by adopting procedures that minimize the need for predicting uncertain events;[8] they lose sight of goals by transforming intermediate means into ultimate ends; and they amplify errors in the content of messages by editing at successive organizational levels (also known as "uncertainty absorption"). Structural flaws—e.g., too few paths to analyze and communicate information—create tension between the organization's structure (the body of knowledge encoded in its hierarchy and rules) and its function (the set of operations). Operations continually produce surprises and anomalies—which we recognize as errors—because the organization's knowledge base is inadequate. Of course, any body of knowledge encoded in organizational structure must fall short of the "real" state of nature that has not yet been presented. Nevertheless, policy makers and organizational designers must surely prefer that their organizations adapt to new conditions rather than remain in the initial design state and that their organizational processes are influenced by their experiences rather than by unproven claims about the future.

---

[8]Richard M. Cyert and James G. March, *A Behavioral Theory of the Firm* (Englewood Cliffs, NJ: Prentice-Hall, 1963), 102.

Simply exhorting organizations to change or to anticipate the future, however, accomplishes little. One goal of this book, therefore, is to identify the elements necessary to design a strategy to tranform the present military into a twenty-first-century RMA military. An RMA military will be composed of multiple, overlapping generations of equipment and ideas—many existing weapons systems, habits and patterns of thought, and organizations will remain well into the twenty-first century. The first step in devising a transformation strategy is to recognize the role of history, or "path dependence," in managing the transformation from present to future.

Path Dependence

In *Through the Looking-Glass and What Alice Found There*, the White Queen instructed Alice on the advantage of memory working both ways. When Alice admitted that her memory worked only one way, the Queen replied, "it's a poor sort of memory that only works backwards."[9] Historian Elting E. Morison modified Lewis Carroll's view by noting that it is a "poor sort of past that only deals with what has happened."[10] Morison recognized the continuing impact of the past on the future.[11] More important, he recognized that history offers military analysts and policy makers the raw experience to test the implicit theories, models, and assumptions that guide the creation of future capabilities.

---

[9]Lewis Carroll, *Through the Looking-Glass and What Alice Found There*, in *More Annotated Alice*, with notes by Martin Gardner (New York: Random House, 1990), 234.

[10]Elting E. Morison, *Men, Machines, and Modern Times* (Cambridge, MA: MIT Press, 1966), 68.

[11]Douglass C. North, "The Paradox of the West," in *The Origins of Modern Freedom in the West*, ed. R. Davis (Stanford, CA: Stanford University Press, 1995), 2; Herbert A. Simon, "Human Nature in Politics: The Dialogue of Psychology with Political Science," *American Political Science Review* 79 (June 1985): 301.

Economic historians use the concept of "path dependence" to trace the influence of the past on the present and future.[12] While a great deal about path dependence is not understood well,[13] the concept focuses attention on identifying important variables and charting their effects over time on societies and economies. This idea is key to analyzing the success or failure of social systems and economies in altering their competitive positions. As such, path dependence offers an analogy with which to evaluate the success or failure of militaries in identifying and exploiting the technological and organizational components of a military revolution.

Economist Paul David defines a path dependent sequence of economic change as one in which "important influences upon the eventual outcome can be exerted by temporally remote events, including happenings dominated by chance elements rather than systematic forces."[14] The history of how the QWERTY layout of the typewriter keyboard gained widespread acceptance illustrates some aspects of path dependence that also apply to the introduction and exploitation of new military technology. David argues that it was by no means clear that the QWERTY layout would succeed when Christopher L. Sholes's patent application was filed in October 1867. Beginning in the

---

[12]Douglass C. North, "Epilogue: Economic Performance through Time," in *Empirical Studies in Institutional Change*, eds. Lee J. Alston, Thrainn Eggertsson, and Douglass C. North (Cambridge: Cambridge University Press, 1996), 349; Douglass C. North, "Where Have We Been and Where Are We Going?" 1996, ftp://wueconb .wustl.edu/econwp/eh/papers/9612/9612001.pdf.

[13]Douglass C. North, "Some Fundamental Puzzles in Economic History/Development," in *The Economy as an Evolving Complex System II*, eds. W. Brian Arthur, Steven N. Durlauf, and David A. Lane (Reading, MA: Addison-Wesley, 1997), 228.

[14]Paul A. David, "Clio and the Economics of QWERTY," *American Economics Review* 75 (May 1985): 332–337; W. Brian Arthur, Yuri Ermoliev, and Yuri Kaniovski, "Path-Dependent Processes and the Emergence of Macrostructure," in *Increasing Returns and Path Dependence in the Economy*, by W. Brian Arthur (Ann Arbor: University of Michigan Press, 1994), 33.

1880s, typewriter-keyboard designs competitive with the QWERTY layout proliferated. However, in the late 1880s the advent of touch typing—an advance over the four-finger "hunt-and-peck" method—began to affect the diffusion of the QWERTY keyboard. As more people learned to touch-type using the QWERTY keyboard, the overall user costs of the keyboard decreased. And as the QWERTY configuration gained acceptance relative to other keyboards, system-level economies of scale led to de facto standardization—or "lock-in" on the QWERTY keyboard. It became too expensive and difficult for consumers to learn another keyboard and reequip the vast numbers of typewriters (and now computers) with an alternative layout.

This historic episode illustrates a generalization about diffusion of innovation that is relevant to military revolutions: when the number of people who own and use a particular form of technology increases, the skills to use that form of technology become more widely distributed and interaction economies grow. There is a strong tendency to make a popular technology standard, and it becomes locked in. Yet, there is no guarantee that the standard technology is better than others in performing a set of tasks. Indeed, the typewriter industry prematurely standardized on the wrong system (other keyboard layouts, e.g., the DVORAK system, allow faster typing), and decentralized decision making (of individuals and businesses that owned typewriters) upheld the decision.

When a new technology appears, which of the many possible variants and diverse applications will succeed is uncertain. Different technologies are tried. Following a period of time and competition, one or more of the new technological forms dominates the others. But market forces may not generate efficient outcomes; even though the new technology has achieved widespread use, it is not necessarily optimal.[15] With respect to military revolutions, the QWERTY layout case history suggests that the typical "vision" documents that attempt to standardize technologies are premature and misconceived. A better approach to ensure the future effectiveness of combat organizations would be (1) to diffuse an experimental attitude to the application of technology and operations throughout the military services, (2) to conduct experiments that challenge military service core missions and platforms, and (3) to pay high-level attention to the development of an effective organizational self-correcting capability.[16] (These issues are examined in chapter 7.) In addition, senior Department of Defense (DOD) leaders should continually emphasize to Congress the necessity of earmarking sufficient funds and personnel to conduct experiments.[17]

Economic historians have used the path dependence concept to caution against wild optimism in proposals that promise radical and quick improvement in the performance of an econ-

---

[15]Richard R. Nelson, "Economic Growth via the Coevolution of Technology and Institutions," in *Evolutionary Economics and Chaos Theory*, eds. Loet Leydesdorff and Peter Van den Besselaar (New York: St. Martin's Press, 1994), 24–25; Arthur, Ermoliev, and Kaniovski, "Path-Dependent Processes and the Emergence of Macrostructure," 46; see also David, "Clio and the Economics of QWERTY"; Joseph Farrell and Garth Saloner, "Installed Base and Compatibility: Innovation, Product Preannouncements, and Predation," *American Economic Review* 76 (December 1986): 940–955.

[16]Martin Landau, "On the Concept of a Self-Correcting Organization," *Public Administration Review* 33 (November/December 1973): 53–42; Mark D. Mandeles, *The Development of the B-52 and Jet Propulsion: A Case Study in Organizational Innovation* (Maxwell AFB, AL: Air University Press, 1998), 41–43.

[17]Conducting a program of experiments assumes the effort to cumulate experimental results over time. In 1999 Congress created a program of joint military experimentation at the U.S. Atlantic Command as a way to support innovation. Now called the Joint Forces Command, it has been hobbled by budget cuts and staffing delays. See Robert Holzer, "U.S. Military Experimentation Program Slow to Take Shape," *Defense News* 14 (14 June 1999): 22.

omy.[18] But path dependence does not explain how an economy started on a particular "path." Individual social, economic, and military systems differ in the extent to which they are sensitive to chance events or "initial conditions" (as arbitrarily defined by an analyst). Historically, military services have resisted abrupt and discontinuous change. While there is a great deal of conjecture about the causal factors for this resistance, path dependence sets an appropriate framework for analysis of the problem. A path dependence analysis is not a simple extrapolation of current trends that transient events can easily overturn; rather it focuses attention on the many systemic—and sometimes, changing—social or political factors (such as coordination costs in changing an information-processing technology) that structure and constrain individual and organizational choices.[19]

Path Dependence and Institutions. To elucidate initial conditions for particular paths, Nobel laureate Douglass North argues that institutions—the formal and informal rules that structure decision making—play a key role in defining the initial economic and social opportunities.[20] Institutions guide the way societies evolve and determine the kinds of organizations that arise. For example, the laws and rules that reward productive economic activity created conditions in the West whereby partnerships and firms could emerge and succeed.[21] An example

---

[18]North, "The Paradox of the West," 7.

[19]See David S. Landes, *The Unbound Prometheus* (London: Cambridge University Press, 1969); David S. Landes, *The Wealth and Poverty of Nations* (New York: W. W. Norton, 1999).

[20]Douglass C. North, *Institutions, Institutional Change, and Economic Performance* (New York: Cambridge University Press, 1990), 3–9.

[21]North, "The Paradox of the West," 7; North, "Some Fundamental Puzzles in Economic History/Development," 225.

of the impact of institutions more directly relevant to national security concerns U.S. vulnerability to cyberwar. In recent conferences, industry spokesmen have argued that the United States is vulnerable to cyberwar not because of its dependence on computer systems but because of its institutions: the private-public division of responsibility for the provision of public goods (e.g., electricity) and the legal restraints on computer-network monitoring.[22] Countries with much closer ties between government and commercial sectors—e.g., the United Kingdom, Germany, Sweden, the Netherlands, and Singapore—are more likely to coordinate faster government-business responses to cyberattacks.[23]

Economic historian Avner Greif found systematic differences in North African Islamic and Venetian trading societies traceable to contrasting beliefs about the role of the individual and institutions in society.[24] Like China, the Islamic world was an early candidate for sustained economic growth. Its people possessed technological, architectural, literary, and scientific skills. At its peak, the Arab Empire exceeded the size of the Roman Empire, remaining a military threat to the West as late as the seventeenth century. But, with only a few exceptions, the belief structure of the Islamic world mitigated intellectual evolution.[25] As historian William McNeill writes, "by a curious and

---

[22]Robert O'Harrow Jr., "Justice Dept. Pushes for Power to Unlock PC Security Systems," *Washington Post*, 20 August 1999, A1, A28.

[23]George I. Seffers, "Nations Seek Defense against Cyber Attack," *Defense News* 14 (9 August 1999): 6, 8.

[24]Avner Greif, "Reputation and Coalition in Medieval Trade: Evidence on the Maghribi Traders," *Journal of Economic History* 49 (1989): 857–882; Avner Greif, "Cultural Beliefs and the Organization of Society: Historical and Theoretical Reflections on Collectivist and Individualist Societies," *Journal of Political Economy* 102 (October 1994): 912–950; Albert O. Hirschman, "Ideology: Mask or Nessus Shirt?" in *Comparison of Economic Systems*, ed. Alexander Eckstein (Berkeley: University of California Press, 1971).

[25]North, "The Paradox of the West," 7.

fateful coincidence, Moslem thought froze into a fixed mold just at the time when intellectual curiosity was awakening in Western Europe—the twelfth and thirteenth centuries."[26]

In Western thought, we find a convergence of arguments from economics, political science, and philosophy of science regarding the impact of epistemological assumptions embedded in institutions on the behaviors of individuals and organizations.[27] The language of these expressions is not always consistent, but the common thread is the long-term effect of institutional rules on individual and social behavior. Operations research analyst Russell L. Ackoff and philosopher of science Sir Karl R. Popper separately argue that unconscious assumptions about the growth of knowledge may affect conceptions of politics—and therefore organizational designs.[28] For instance, in *Federalist Papers 51*, James Madison argues that government is "the greatest of all reflections on human nature." In effect, he turned the classic problem of designing "good" government on its head. Instead of searching for good, wise, or just rulers, Madison asked how to prevent—or at least minimize—"bad" government. Since people's ideas about the world are fallible,

---

[26]William H. McNeill, *The Rise of the West: A History of the Human Community* (New York: New American Library, 1963); see also Landes, *The Wealth and Poverty of Nations*, 392–415; Bernard Lewis, *What Went Wrong?* (Oxford: Oxford University Press, 2002).

[27]I believe that future formalization of the argument about the growth of knowledge may avoid the following three main obstacles to predicting the effects of constitutional-level rule changes over a long period: (1) the interests of people change more rapidly than changes in constitutional rules, (2) strategies change as a result of rule changes, and (3) rules don't operate in isolation. How a change in one rule will affect incentives and behavior over time depends on the configuration of rules in that set. This creates a calculation problem: the large number of single rules that can be altered and the great variety of rule configurations make the total number of possibilities very large. When interaction effects exist among the rules, studying changes of one or a few rules in isolation is difficult.

[28]Russell L. Ackoff, "A Revolution in Organizational Concepts," *Naval War College Review* 24 (June 1972): 4; Karl R. Popper, *Conjectures and Refutations: The Growth of Scientific Knowledge* (New York: Harper Torchbooks, 1963), 4–5.

the answer lay in the arrangement of government offices (and elections) to identify and correct errors.[29] The U.S. Constitution reflected Madison's understanding of individual and institutional relationships, and incorporated what biophysicist John R. Platt describes as "stabilization feedbacks" by establishing a system of economic and social prosperity.[30]

The role of institutions in structuring decisions and decision making has three implications for the understanding of military revolutions in the United States. First, the same institutions can generate parallel groupings of organizations and alternate sets of behaviors. During the interwar period, the Army and Navy operated under the same institutional rules as other government bodies—i.e., the checks and balances and separation of powers embodied in the U.S. Constitution. The naval aviation community (but not the naval munitions/torpedo community) was able to exploit these formal institutional rules by creating an interactive relationship among the General Board, the fleet, the Naval War College, and the Bureau of Aeronautics.[31] The primary effect of this multiorganizational arrangement was that the naval aviation community identified and reduced uncertainties in developing technology and operational concepts for the employment of aircraft carriers. Some early technological-operational options favored by high-level persons were rejected and not locked in, e.g., Rear Adm. William A. Moffett's preference for the use of airships. In contrast, the Army—not operating with an analogous set of organizations and patterns of interaction—was unable to identify and exploit the potential operational ad-

[29]James Madison, "Number 51," *The Federalist Papers* (New York: Mentor Book, 1961), 322.

[30]John Rader Platt, *The Step to Man* (New York: John Wiley and Sons, 1970), 109–110.

[31]Thomas C. Hone, Norman Friedman, and Mark D. Mandeles, *American and British Aircraft Carrier Development, 1919–1941* (Annapolis, MD: Naval Institute Press, 1999).

vantages of mechanized warfare and tanks.[32] In noting the failure of the *Journal of the U.S. Cavalry Association* to pay attention to mechanization, Edward L. Katzenbach observed, "one cannot help but be impressed with the intellectual isolation" of the Army in the 1930s.[33]

Second, institutions and organizations can enhance prospects for success or hinder the achievement of an RMA. Efficient economic organizations are rare. Similarly, military organizations and patterns of interaction that can identify and exploit potentially revolutionary technologies and operational concepts are an exception among the many military organizations that deal with acquisition and operations.

Third, the institutions and organizations that exist when a potential military innovation appears and is refined for combat exert a powerful influence over the types of knowledge required for exploitation of the innovation, the types of knowledge generated from its exploitation, and the evolutionary path followed by the technology and associated operational concepts.

The imagery of revolution, which assumes speedy and profound changes, is partly responsible for attempts to identify the single origin of a military revolution. The historical identification of an initial event or technology that led to a great change is largely arbitrary, especially since—with the exception of nuclear weapons—it is the *accumulated* decisions or events that produce an abrupt change in military capabilities, that is, a military revolution. Did the information revolution begin with Alexander Graham Bell's 1876 invention of the telephone, Gugliemo Marconi's 1895 invention of wireless telegraphy, or the work in the early twentieth century of the great American Telephone and Telegraph engineer Harry Nyquist? Or did the

---

[32]See Mandeles, *The Development of the B-52 and Jet Propulsion*, 34–37.

[33]Edward L. Katzenbach Jr., "The Horse Cavalry in the Twentieth Century: A Study in Policy Response," in *American Defense Policy*, 3rd edition, eds. Richard G. Head and Ervin J. Rokke (Baltimore: Johns Hopkins University Press, 1973), 419.

seminal 1948 paper by Claude E. Shannon, "A Mathematical Theory of Communication," mark the start of the revolution? Did the revolution begin only with the 1948 invention of the transistor by J. Bardeen, W. H. Brattain, and W. Shockley?

Indeed, the information revolution is based on three sets of technological developments. The first technology was the invention of communication machines: the telephone, wireless telegraphy, radio, and television. The second technology was observation instruments: devices that measure, observe, and record the properties of events and objects, such as the pressure gauge, ohmmeter, and speedometer. These devices generate symbols or data that may be transmitted with the first technology. The final technology was the digital electronic computer, which could manipulate symbols logically. Together, these three technologies make it possible to mechanize mental work by observing objects and events, communicating about them, and manipulating symbols for objects and events very rapidly.[34] Thus, the accumulation of discoveries, inventions, and theories—each important in the growth of knowledge and technologies—produced an information revolution.

The development and exploitation of these technologies create new problems, questions, and technologies relevant to military operations. Analyses of military revolutions are uselessly preoccupied with identifying origins of a complex of technologies and operational concepts. The understandable hope behind such analyses is to create universally applicable guidelines for the early adoption of revolutionary technologies, thus shortening developmental timelines and making the entire process cheaper. The effort, unfortunately, is misconceived. No methodology can be devised to make correct predictions consistently about such matters.[35]

---

[34]Ackoff, "A Revolution in Organizational Concepts," 7–8.
[35]Karl R. Popper, *The Poverty of Historicism* (New York: Harper Torchbooks, 1964).

Two related issues affect the application of the path dependence concept to military revolutions: (1) the impact of social structure on organizational design and (2) the knowledge gleaned from experience and inferences made from small samples (e.g., historical events). These issues will be considered in turn.

Impact of Social Structure

In one respect, a concern with the historical origin of a complex of technologies, operational concepts, and organizations may yield useful insights into particular features of that complex. Organizations formed during one historical period typically have different social structures from those formed during another period,[36] and an organization's original structural characteristics appear to persist from the time of its invention.[37] The pyramid-shaped hierarchical structure of today's railroad organizations, invented in the nineteenth century, is much different from the flat structure of late-twentieth-century software design firms. Furthermore, some organizational forms could not be invented until the social conditions appropriate to them had been created. In the eighteenth and nineteenth centuries, for instance, mass armies could not have been created, maintained, and moved without the widespread literacy necessary for administrative tasks. At the dawn of the twenty-first century, the proliferation of information-processing and calculational tools may provide the social conditions for new organizational forms. These conditions may include officers and enlisted personnel with (1) high literacy and numeracy, (2) skills in operating all sorts of modern computer, communications, and

[36]W. Brian Arthur, "Increasing Returns and the New World of Business," *Harvard Business Review* 74 (July/August 1996): 100.

[37]Arthur L. Stinchcombe, "Social Structure and Organizations," in *Handbook of Organizations*, ed. James G. March (Chicago: Rand McNally, 1965), 154–159.

electronic equipment, and (3) a practiced ability to innovate to achieve high-level objectives.

A favorable social structure is a necessary but insufficient condition, however, for the elaboration of information revolution–based military capabilities. If these twenty-first-century social conditions are applicable to military organizations, the structure and operational modes of future RMA combat organizations may look very different from the twentieth century's peacetime military organizations for training, acquiring, and equipping. Indeed, it may be necessary to separate military departments more fully from yet-to-be-created RMA-type combat commands and to organize these future combat component commands under different principles. (This topic will be revisited in chapter 6.)

Small Samples: Inferences and Learning

Logicians' and philosophers' objections to inferring valid lawlike generalizations from individual historical events are relevant to learning in military organizations. History offers only small samples of combat experience. There are at least five practical difficulties in learning about, and making inferences from, these small samples. First, learning and making inferences from historical samples are difficult cognitive tasks because events are produced by complex combinations of factors. It is not always clear, even with hindsight, just what a previous war or battle proved. The problem of representing and interpreting experience—this battle or war is an example of what complex of factors?—persists throughout the historiography of military operations. Modern war is composed of a series of battles, rather than a single defining clash of forces. The application of a doctrine or operational concept in one location or period may not produce the same valued outcome—victory—at some other time or place. The passage of time worsens this obstacle. Long lag times between actions and outcomes—even assuming that outcome feedback is unambiguous—obscure causal connections.[38]

Second, in unstable or fast-moving environments, people and organizations may learn more slowly than the environment changes. In such situations, what is learned quickly becomes no longer relevant to the problems faced. Third, people or organizations may learn false lessons or have exaggerated and unwarranted confidence in their historical understandings. Fourth, learning about immediate problems may interfere with learning about deeper, more distant and elusive problems. Finally, problems that result from limited memory, conflict among personnel, turnover, and low centralization are difficult to extract lessons from.[39]

Experience may be a poor teacher not only because of the complex and changing nature of the world in which learning takes place but also because various actors are learning simultaneously based on their own unique experiences. Organizational subunits may learn quite effectively when separated and buffered from headquarters, but several interacting subunits can find it very difficult to learn simultaneously in a noisy environment. As organization theorists Daniel Levinthal and James March argue, "learning from experience involves inferences from information. It involves memory. It involves pooling personal experience with knowledge gained from the experiences

---

[38]James G. March, Lee S. Sproull, and Michal Tamuz, "Learning from Samples of One or Fewer," in *Organizational Learning*, eds. Michael D. Cohen and Lee S. Sproull (Thousand Oaks, CA: Sage Publications, 1996), 3.

[39]Daniel A. Levinthal and James G. March, "The Myopia of Learning," special issue, *Strategic Management Journal* 14 (Winter 1993): 97.

of others."[40] It is very difficult to learn effectively from a confusing experience. And "friction" and the "fog of war" make the war experience confusing, even with hindsight.

Viewing history as small samples of unique occurrences overlooks the variety of experience that is represented in each historical event.[41] Organizations may augment their analyses of history (and of exercises and experiments) by developing and analyzing their experience from multiple levels. People at different levels of an organization experience events and the consequences of action diversely. Civilian organizations learn from experience when people propose and install new formal rules: problems are identified differently; the order in which tasks are considered and executed may change; and plans are devised to handle newly perceived or different situations. As we will see in chapter 4, Gulf War air leaders did not appreciate these factors and underestimated the effects of last-minute air-tasking order changes on the squadron pilots' and planners' ability to do their jobs.

Separating What We Know from What We Don't Know

Civilian and military leaders recognize the importance of organization to effectiveness in a general way and often attempt to improve effectiveness through reorganization. Most reorganizations fail to achieve what their public- or private-sector architects hoped. The primary reason for these failures is the poverty of knowledge about how organizations work.[42] In the effort to design or create new RMA-type organizations, many defense

---

[40]Levinthal and March, "The Myopia of Learning," 96–97.

[41]March, Sproull, and Tamuz, "Learning from Samples of One or Fewer," 2.

[42]James Q. Wilson, *Bureaucracy* (New York: Basic Books, 1989), 11–12.

analysts seek inspiration from business firms' experience of doing new things, through either borrowing (e.g., hiring expertise or copying programs) or inventing.[43] Unfortunately, the experiences of business firms may not be readily transferable to military organizations. For example, in a study of Toshiba Corporation, economist W. Mark Fruin describes how company management fosters commercial innovation. But, by linking the factors explaining Toshiba's success to its products, markets, organization, and culture, Fruin renders problematic any generalization about Toshiba's management that could apply to other countries, corporations, or organizations. The Toshiba style of management may be quite rare, even in Japan, where corporations such as NEC, Hitachi, and Mitsubishi each organize the management of their affairs differently.[44] Organization theorist Karl E. Weick observes that knowledge creation by business firms is apt to be firm-specific. The knowledge acquired by business firms is not preserved in abstractions and must be invented anew with each reorganization or problem opportunity. Tinkering and customizing in business firms, in the absence of systematic evaluation, leads to many reorganization failures.[45] Thus, the effort to apply the business experience uncritically to combat operations is an example of false learning.

Academics have not necessarily created better knowledge than their private-sector counterparts. The academic field of organization theory has produced interesting theoretical results, but these have had little application in the real world of administration. As organization theorist James G. March notes, "We

[43]James G. March and Herbert A. Simon, *Organizations* (New York: John Wiley and Sons, 1958), 188; Wesley M. Cohen and Daniel A. Levinthal, "Absorptive Capacity: A New Perspective on Learning and Innovation," *Administrative Science Quarterly* 35 (March 1990): 128.

[44]See W. Mark Fruin, *Knowledge Works: Managing Intellectual Capital at Toshiba* (New York: Oxford University Press, 1997).

[45]Karl E. Weick, "Drop Your Tools: An Allegory for Organizational Studies," *Administrative Science Quarterly* 41 (June 1996): 310.

know more about bounded rationality and the scarcity of attention as theoretical problems than we do about how organizations cope with them. . . . We know more about incremental hill
climbing on an imagined surface using formally specified decision rules (or rules that learn) than we do about problem identification, problem solving, and change in the messy world of real
organizations."[46]

It is clear that there is much more to learn about individuals'
behavior in organizations and about organizational design in
general, including the relationship between organizational
structure and outcomes. Clear attention to the nature of evidence being adduced to support claims, to the limits to generalizations, and to levels of analysis should help distinguish what
we know from what we do not know.

Initial Research Questions

To distinguish what we know from what we don't know about
military revolutions, the research upon which this book is based
initially prompted the following questions:

1. How might a tactical unit, equipped with new sensor and
   communications equipment, operate? How would one
   unit's actions be coordinated with other units?
2. How might a theater commander operate with new sensor and communications equipment?
3. How might organizations and decision makers cope with
   information overflow?
4. How should decision makers trade off tight- and loose-

[46]James G. March, "Administrative Practice, Organization Theory, and Political Philosophy: Ruminations on the *Reflections* of John M. Gaus," *PS: Political Science and
Politics* 30 (December 1997): 692–693.

coupling of collections of organizations? When should decision makers emphasize one or the other?

5. How may we factor and coordinate a large set of necessary decisions so that interactions do not impair achievement of military ends?

6. How may we reduce the complexity of senior commanders' decision problems to manageable proportions?

7. How may we conserve a commander's attention by reducing the number of decision problems he faces?

The next chapter will explore the methodological role of multiple levels of analysis in studies of future military organization. Its point of departure is in the work of Jean de Bloch, the first "scientific" arms controller, whose work identified a military revolution at the turn of the twentieth century.

CHAPTER 3

Levels of Analysis, Trade-offs, and *The Future of War*

The conduct of war is not an exercise in metaphysics—it is a practice. As a practice it involves the use of certain machines, and the pursuit of military ends has always been determined by the inherent potentialities or limitations of the machines with which war is waged.[1]

This chapter focuses on the brilliant and innovative turn-of-the-century analyst Jean de Bloch, whose study of war provides a rare example of the accurate anticipation of new technologies' impact on military operations.[2] Bloch's deductions on tactics and logistics far surpassed those of his contemporaries and treated problems about which no one else thought. He alone questioned the effects of a long, drawn-out war on the ability of civilians to bear great privation and hardship and on the stability of the European social order. He also anticipated the concept of a "war economy," or the relationship of commerce, industry, and agriculture to the military effort.

Bloch's great contribution is his approach to understanding military operations and the relationship among technologies, tactics, and operations. He directs the reader to consider problems that are not immediately obvious. Bloch's approach to the analysis of war at the turn of the twentieth century was remark-

---

[1]Bernard Brodie, *Sea Power in the Machine Age* (Princeton, NJ: Princeton University Press, 1941), 4.

[2]Sir Michael Howard argues that Bloch's study of war, *The Future of War*, is unequaled in "its combination of rigor and scope." See "Men against Fire: Expectations of War in 1914," *International Security* 9 (Summer 1984): 41–57.

ably prescient and has much to teach us about how to engage in similar analysis at the turn of the twenty-first century. Bloch's *The Future of War* was largely based on his painstaking analysis of the development and impact of myriad technological advances in war machinery toward the end of the nineteenth century. Bloch did not have the concept of the RMA available to him, but it would have been apt. Both then and now the immediate intellectual challenge was to understand the future of combat operations in the context of rapid technological change and analytic tools that were inadequate to the task. A second-order intellectual challenge was to discern the larger impacts of this revolution not only on the conduct of war but on society as a whole and on the prospect for peaceful resolution of international conflict. A few words on the RMA concept are necessary to introduce the ensuing discussion of levels of analysis.

The RMA Concept

Borrowing from the Soviets, American military analysts have been discussing the concept of "military-technical revolutions" under the RMA label.[3] Indeed, these analysts have made the RMA a hot topic by observing and describing the state-of-the-art technology that now offers military planners a dazzling array of advanced weapons systems, communications equipment, computer tools, and more. In combination, such ad-

---

[3]See for example N. A. Lomov, ed., *Scientific-Technical Progress and the Revolution in Military Affairs*, trans. U.S. Air Force (Washington, DC: GPO, 1973); "The Revolution in Military Affairs," in *Soviet Military Encyclopedia*, vol. 7 (Moscow: Voyenizdat, 1979), 82; Mary C. FitzGerald, "Advanced Conventional Munitions and Moscow's Defensive Force Posture," *Defense Analysis* 6 (1990): 167–191; FitzGerald, "Soviet Armed Forces after the Gulf War: Demise of the Defensive Doctrine?" *RFE/RL Research Institute* 3 (1991); Peter Schweizer, "The Soviet Military Goes High-Tech," *Orbis* (Spring 1991): 195–218; D. L. Smith and A. L. Meier, "Ogarkov's Revolution: Soviet Military Doctrine for the 1990s," *International Defense Review* 20 (July 1987): 869–873.

vanced systems may provide an order of magnitude increase in combat capability. Noting the Gulf War performance of stealth aircraft, precise long-range conventional munitions, and advanced sensor, targeting, and information-processing technology, many observers suggest that major improvements in combat effectiveness are impending as new technologies are integrated into military forces.[4]

For American analysts, a military revolution occurs not as the result of the deployment of a single new weapon or technology, but when a set of technologies and associated operational concepts transform the nature and character of warfare and military organizations and their personnel are able to deploy and exploit this set of technologies. Such revolutions are marked not only by changes in force structure and in the way armies, navies, and air forces fight but also in the way they are organized and trained. During such revolutions, military professionals themselves are often uncertain about new operational concepts and forms of military organization, a phenomenon that is as true today as it was at the end of the nineteenth century.

How may one recognize incipient military revolutions? How do military professionals know they are living through such a revolution? Are the components of a military revolution clear enough to allow an unequivocal identification by those experiencing it? Imagination alone is insufficient to analyze such

---

[4]See for example John W. Bodnar, "The Military Technical Revolution: From Hardware to Information," *Naval War College Review* 46 (Summer 1993): 7–21; Ashton B. Carter, William J. Perry, and John D. Steinbruner, *A New Concept of Cooperative Security*, Brookings Occasional Papers (Washington, DC: Brookings Institution, 1992), 3, 29–30; James R. FitzSimonds and Jan M. van Tol, "Revolutions in Military Affairs," *Joint Force Quarterly* (Spring 1994): 24–31; Dan Gouré, "Is There a Military-Technical Revolution in America's Future?" *The Washington Quarterly* 16 (Autumn 1993): 179; Richard P. Hallion, *Storm over Iraq: Air Power and the Gulf War* (Washington, DC: Smithsonian Institution Press, 1992); William J. Perry, "Desert Storm and Deterrence," *Foreign Affairs* 70 (Fall 1991): 66; Andrew F. Krepinevich Jr., "Keeping Pace with the Military-Technological Revolution," *Issues in Science and Technology* (Summer 1994): 23–29.

complex phenomena, and military men of great reputation, both in Bloch's time and today, have failed to recognize the nature of the revolution they themselves are experiencing.

Even the Soviets acknowledged that military revolutions usually are identified most clearly with hindsight once critical technologies and tactics have been developed or used.[5] Hindsight makes identification of military revolutions seem easier than it is, because, with hindsight, (1) order is seen in random behavior, (2) confirmatory evidence is counted more heavily than disconfirmatory evidence, and (3) memory is selective and limited.[6] Thus, the many military ideas and technologies that were *not* implemented because they were unworkable are forgotten. A classic example is the prediction of Theodore von Kármán's Army Air Forces Scientific Advisory Board Report, which considered nuclear propulsion viable for aircraft.[7] The effort to develop such aircraft was very costly and finally abandoned.[8] Indeed, there are very few cases of prescient forecasting of military revolutions; most cases probably occur in the realm of science fiction, and even there wrong guesses predominate.[9] At a

---

[5]The problem of choosing the best military technology (when it is in its infancy) is analogous to the problems confronted by U.S. economists acting as policy analysts. Economist Richard R. Nelson notes that economists often believed that with good analysis they could reliably choose *ex ante* the best program or option from a set of alternatives. Yet experience showed that there was seldom enough *ex ante* information to make a proper decision. Richard R. Nelson, "Issues and Suggestions for the Study of Industrial Organization in a Regime of Rapid Technical Change," in *Policy Issues and Research Opportunities in Industrial Organization in a Regime of Rapid Technical Change*, ed. Victor Fuchs (New York: Columbia University Press, 1972), 49.

[6]See Daniel Kahneman, Paul Slovic, and Amos Tversky, eds., *Judgment under Uncertainty: Heuristics and Biases* (Cambridge: Cambridge University Press, 1982).

[7]Theodore von Kármán, *Toward New Horizons: A Report to General of the Army H. H. Arnold*, 15 December 1945; unpublished report.

[8]Mark D. Mandeles, "The Air Force's Management of R&D: Redundancy in the B-52 and B-70 Development Programs" (Ph.D. dissertation, Indiana University, 1985), chap. 4.

[9]Isaac Asimov, in *Foundation* (New York: Doubleday, 1951), foresaw the military potential of computers and the miniaturization of electronics, weapons, and sensors;

minimum, the predominance of incorrect forecasts should make policy makers reluctant to foreclose technological and operational options in the absence of alternatives. The watchword of all those concerned about the RMA should be parallel development is necessary because it provides alternatives; in the long run, it's also cheaper.[10]

The ease with which military revolutions are seen in hindsight perpetuates the problem that bedevils military (and social) analysis today as it did in the 1890s: preoccupation with causality at just one level of analysis. Bloch's brilliance was in recognizing the need for multiple levels of analysis. With respect to military revolutions, three types of cause come into play, not just one. Analysis must address, first, the set of technologies that allows tasks to be accomplished; second, the organizational matters of tactics and operational concepts, wherein people cooperate and coordinate their actions to achieve military ends; and finally, the actions and behaviors of people and organizations making up the governing regimes of nation-states. Moreover, these factors—technologies, tactics and operational concepts, and regimes—interact. Any explanation of military revolutions that ignores these three levels and their interactions is certain to misrepresent the complexity and implications of a military revolution.

In a few cases, military leaders have realized that they were living through a military revolution, but their ability to act on their knowledge and convictions was constrained by (1) the po-

---

his thoughts about robotics stimulated a whole generation. In a personal communication, Col. David A. Anhalt (USAF) added that Arthur C. Clarke foresaw the utility of satellites in his fiction and nonfiction writing. Clarke also explored other concepts, such as asymmetric warfare, that have captured the imagination of many military writers. In the 1951 short story "Superiority," Clarke describes a military defeat due to the "inferior science of our armies." See Arthur C. Clarke, *Expedition to Earth* (New York: Ballantine Books, 1965).

[10]Richard R. Nelson, "Uncertainty, Learning, and the Economics of Parallel Research and Development Efforts," *Review of Economics and Statistics* 43 (November 1961): 351–364.

litical institutions and practices of their nations, (2) the rate of technological change at the time, and (3) the magnitude of organizational changes needed to implement the new ideas and technologies. Emperor Napoleon III of France, for instance, recognized the enormous advantage of rapid-firing, long-range infantry weapons. Yet, he was more concerned with protecting the secret of the crank-operated machine gun, the Montigny *mitrailleuse*, than with developing appropriate tactics and doctrine defining the gun's use.[11] Given his authority, his concern became official policy. As a result, when the revolutionary machine gun was finally deployed in 1870, the officers and troops of his own army did not know how to use it effectively.[12] They had been undone by the politics and character of Napoleon's regime and the absence of organizations to analyze the gun and to integrate it into the military.

Bloch's Analysis of Warfare

Prior to the mid-nineteenth century, officers could master the tools and tactics of a military career and not ever conceive that such matters would change drastically over their lifetimes. As Bernard Brodie noted,

> When Admiral Nelson was killed at Trafalgar in 1804 aboard the flagship *Victory*, the ship was then forty years old. Of course it had to be rebuilt several times because of rotting tim-

---

[11]John Ellis, *The Social History of the Machine Gun* (New York: Pantheon Books, 1975), 63.

[12]The *mitrailleuse* presented a bundle of twenty-five barrels; each detonated sequentially by turning a handle. It had a range of almost two thousand yards and a firing rate of 150 rounds per minute. Michael Howard, *The Franco-Prussian War: The German Invasion of France, 1870–1871* (London: Granada, 1979), 36. See also Alex Roland's analysis of how a regime's goal of maintaining the secrecy of a weapons system may prevent its exploitation in combat. Alex Roland, "Secrecy, Technology, and War: Greek Fire and the Defense of Byzantium, 678–1204," *Technology and Culture* 33 (October 1992): 661.

bers, but it was the same ship in design, and it had exactly the same guns that it carried for forty years, smoothbore 32-pounders which fired only solid, round shot. Thus, Admiral Nelson could learn his trade and exploit it without fearing that technology would take the ground out from under his feet.[13]

However, by the mid-nineteenth century, the rate of military and nonmilitary invention began advancing more quickly, and these changes altered the amount and types of knowledge required for military command. Concurrently, Bloch's interest in the effects of war on Warsaw was stimulated by his participation in the transportation of troops and supplies for the Russo-Turkish War of 1877–1878. As an industrialist and entrepreneur, Bloch was skilled at economic planning and applied his economic perspective to the rapid advances in military and relevant nonmilitary technologies.[14] He was amazed that military professionals—high-ranking officers—overlooked these technological developments.[15] Bloch inferred propositions about tactics, operations, and the home front from his awareness of the manifold impacts of the industrial revolution on European societies, from historical analysis, and from military experiments. In effect, Bloch identified an on-going military revolution—a set of technologies, weapons, tactics, and organizational structures—that had transformed the nature and character of warfare and the impact of war on society.[16]

---

[13]Bernard Brodie, "Introductory Remarks," in *Science, Technology, and Warfare*, eds. Monte D. Wright and Lawrence J. Paszek (Washington, DC: GPO, 1970), 85.

[14]Jean de Bloch, *The Work of the Peace Societies: How to Widen Their Programme* (Edinburgh: "Observer" Works, Chatham, 1901), 6.

[15]Jean de Bloch, "The Wars of the Future," *Contemporary Review* 80, no. 429 (September 1901): 305.

[16]Of course, Bloch did not work alone. He had numerous contacts with senior military theorists in several countries, and he set up a research institute—in modern terms, a "think tank"—at the corner of Krolewska and Marszalkowska Streets in Warsaw and gathered prominent scholars to work at this institute, including Nahum

For military analysts of the late nineteenth century, Jean de
Bloch was an unlikely and unwanted Cassandra. The Christian
convert from Judaism served successfully as a railroad entrepreneur, banker, and Russian state councilor, but he never served
as a soldier nor did he possess any other military experience.[17]
Bloch undertook an in-depth study of the available descriptions
and analyses of military operations and discussed his conclusions with officers from many countries. He reported that these
officers generally agreed with his conclusions about military
operations—but not the implications of war for the home front
and the economy.[18] He pointedly noted that the civilian who
criticizes military policy is

> "frowned down as an impertinent busybody, and perhaps
> talked of as a friend of his country's foes. Even the citizen
> who has devoted himself with success to the study of military
> science . . . is rudely told that the ground he treds is holy and
> reserved for the initiated. It is thus that the Army is wrapped
> up in swaddling clothes and protected from the light of the
> day. Yet the donning of the military uniform is hardly a sacra-
> mental act which confers divine grace and deep insight upon
> the many who are called to it."[19]

The European political and military officials Bloch at-
tempted to influence planned and argued largely on the basis of
what Nobel laureate Herbert A. Simon has called "a closed set
of variables." That is, the representations of reality that in-

Sokolow, Samuel Adalberg, and Isaac Leib Peretz. Nahum Sokolow, "Jan Bloch: The
Loyal Convert," in *The Golden Tradition: Jewish Life and Thought in Eastern Eu-
rope*, ed. Lucy S. Dawidowicz (Boston: Beacon Press, 1967), 344. Christopher Bel-
lamy cites the *Soviet Military Encyclopedia* (1976–1980); see Bellamy's "'Civilian
Experts' and Russian Defense Thinking: The Renewed Relevance of Jan Bloch,"
RUSI Journal 137 (April 1992): 51.

[17]Mark D. Mandeles, "Jean de Bloch and *The Future of War*," paper presented to the
Military Classics Seminar, Washington, DC, 16 January 1990.

[18]Jean de Bloch, *The Future of War in its Technical, Economic and Political Relations*
(Boston: Ginn, 1902), xii.

[19]Bloch, "The Wars of the Future," 309.

formed analyses and decisions of senior diplomatic and military officials were fixed, and the institutions in which they served were not structured to permit open criticism of existing policy or to provide competing views.[20] Public debate about new weapons technology in some democratic countries (e.g., new forms of artillery in Great Britain or steam propulsion for the post–Civil War American Navy[21]) played an important but not decisive role in adoption or rejection of those technologies. Public opinion in itself could not break officials out of the "closed set of variables" from which they thought about, planned for, and waged war.

Bloch argued that the modern technology of arms design in 1898 substantially increased the lethality and power of defense.[22] In particular, the magazine rifle, smokeless powder (introduced in 1886), flat-trajectory bullet, smaller rifle bore (increasing the penetration of bullets), quick-firing artillery, and high-explosive artillery shells would create a fire-swept zone (of approximately one thousand meters) making a frontal assault against an entrenched defense suicidal.[23] This zone could

---

[20]Edward L. Katzenbach Jr., "The Horse Cavalry in the Twentieth Century: A Study in Policy Response," in *American Defense Policy*, 3rd edition, eds. Richard G. Head and Ervin J. Rokke (Baltimore: Johns Hopkins University Press, 1973), 411.

[21]Public debates in newspapers about the effectiveness of guns designed by Sir William Armstrong and Joseph Whitworth played an important role in the British government's choice of Armstrong's design, and Armstrong understood the importance of public opinion as filtered through newspapers. Marshall J. Bastable, "From Breechloaders to Monster Guns: Sir William Armstrong and the Invention of Modern Artillery, 1854–1880," *Technology and Culture* 33 (April 1992): 239. For information about post–Civil War steam-propulsion technology, see Frank M. Bennett, *The Steam Navy of the United States* (Westport, CT: Greenwood Press, 1972), 514–550, esp. 526.

[22]Bloch, *The Future of War*, xvii–xxv, 17–24, 338; Bloch, "The Transvaal War: Its Lessons in Regard to Militarism and Army Reorganization, part 1," *Journal of the Royal United Service Institution* 45 (November 1901): 1320–1321; Bloch, *The Work of the Peace Societies*, 15–22; Bloch, "Militarism and Lord Roberts' Army Reorganization Scheme," *Contemporary Review* 80 (December 1901): 761–792.

[23]For an analysis of the ballistic properties of smoothbore weapons, see Bert S. Hall, *Weapons and Warfare in Renaissance Europe* (Baltimore: Johns Hopkins University

be crossed but only if the attacking forces had a numerical advantage of eight to one, a number Bloch derived from his analysis of actual operations in the 1877–1878 Russo-Turkish War
and the 1870–1871 Franco-Prussian War and from his own experiments in Switzerland.[24]

Bloch's significant predictions derive from the nature of the
fire-swept zone. He inferred that opposing armies would be entrenched and separated and that wars would become long inde-
cisive siegelike affairs.[25] He was pessimistic about the ability of
the modern city-dwelling soldier to long endure under-siege
conditions,[26] and thought that a great number of soldiers would
be lost to sickness and exhaustion and that care for the
wounded would deteriorate.[27] In support of his arguments,
Bloch cited an unnamed British army physician, who declared
it would be necessary in a continental war "to have as many
hospital attendants as there are soldiers in the fighting line."[28]
In fact, Bloch noted that the dead and dying would be used "as
ramparts to strengthen the shelter trenches. This was actually
done at the battle of Worth, where Dr. Porth, chief military
physician of the Bavarian army, reported . . . ramparts built up
of soldiers who had fallen by the side of their comrades."[29]

In addition, Bloch predicted an increase in the problems of
logistics and maneuver on the battlefield. Large armies would
be composed primarily of civilians and reserves, not "veterans

---

Press, 1997). Hall's work shows how the lethality of weapons increased markedly in
a relatively short period of approximately forty years, as rifled replaced smoothbore
weapons.

[24]Jean de Bloch, "South Africa and Europe," *The North American Review* 174 (April
1902): 497.

[25]For example, see Bloch, "The Wars of the Future," 320; and Bloch, *The Future of
War*, xvi, 331–333.

[26]Bloch, *The Future of War*, 340.

[27]Ibid., xli, 152.

[28]Ibid., xli.

[29]Ibid., xli.

accustomed to act together," and thus they would be harder to direct and control.[30] Three effects of the size of armies bear mention. First, the difficulty of troop control during battle would increase the number of casualties among officers, who would be compelled to expose themselves to supervise and direct men.[31] Bloch added that, in his conversations with military officers, the Germans and Austro-Hungarians knew they would probably die; the French officers did not believe it, but, Bloch predicted, they would find out.[32] The increased casualties taken by experienced officers meant that, in relatively short order, inexperienced officers would lead the army. This observation led Bloch to ask: "How is war to be fought if the experienced officers are killed—who will lead and prevent a breakdown of army organization?"[33] Second, the large size of armies would translate into increased demand for the great variety of materiel needed to conduct operations, e.g., food, fodder for animals, ammunition, weapons, and replacement soldiers. The increased demand for materiel from the home front would also stress the national transportation system. Finally, the new weapons technologies combined with mass-conscription armies and railroad-generated strategic mobility would transform warfare from the maneuver of forces into a long-term stalemate decided by attrition and economic exhaustion of the continental powers.[34]

For Bloch, this analysis of warfare at the tactical and operational levels had clear implications for nation-states. He recognized that war entails a national effort. He argued that armies would no longer be composed of "gallant, jovial cavaliers, but of entire peoples who curse the fate that compels them to aban-

[30]Ibid., xxxii.

[31]Ibid., xxxiv.

[32]Ibid., xxxv; see also Michael Howard, *War in European History* (London: Oxford University Press, 1976), 105–106.

[33]Bloch, *The Future of War*, xxxii, xxxv, 335.

[34]Ibid., xvi, xlii–xlix.

don their trades, industries, and professions."[35] The economic effect of a continental war would extend beyond the borders of the belligerents. All "nations are likewise affected by the stagnation of trade and the slackness of industry."[36] Bloch added that if it were possible, on technical grounds, to wage war as before, "economic considerations put their absolute veto on it, and from this decision there is no appeal."[37] War would involve a multiplication of expenditures necessary to conduct it and a diminution of the sources for that expenditure. Bloch questioned whether the population left behind the fighting men would be able to supply the army with what was needed to carry on the campaign.[38]

Economic and political considerations had fostered increased competition regarding the size of armies on the Continent. The only way to meet the need for larger armies was to conscript more and more men for shorter periods of time, so that, on mobilization, the armies would be filled with trained reserves drawn from civilian life. But, the removal of male workers from the nation's industry would create problems not thought of by military and civilian leaders. Calling up a large number of reserves would deplete industry of its employees, which would lead businesses to close their doors and create a cycle of unemployment. (Bloch did not anticipate that factories would not close in wartime: instead women substituted for men

---

[35]Bloch, "The Wars of the Future," 311. Indeed, Bloch argued, "it is unworthy to regard war from the point of view of a sportsman and to regard an Army as an instrument for seeking adventures and showing address and audacity. Those who regard war in this light had better go hunting lions or competing in championships. The sacrifice of a single life merely in order to show heroism is nothing better than a crime." Bloch, "The Transvaal War: Its Lessons in Regard to Militarism and Army Reorganization, part 2," *Journal of the Royal United Service Institution* 45 (December 1901): 1437.

[36]Bloch, "The Wars of the Future," 311.

[37]Ibid., 321.

[38]Bloch, *The Future of War*, xlii.

in the workplace. Nor did he anticipate the tremendous change in social roles that followed.[39]) The inability of nations either to grow enough food for themselves or for their armies would bring higher prices, which, combined with the absence of workers' earnings, would force large withdrawals from savings institutions. The savings institutions, whose portfolios comprised mainly individual mortgages, would have to foreclose on those mortgages. Securities would fall, and the rich would begin to refuse to make war loans. Ultimately, the nations at war would be forced to issue paper money, and their economies would collapse. As Bloch concluded, "the basis of my argument is that under the military, social, and economic conditions of Europe at the present day, though it is quite possible that war may break out, it is almost impossible for it to be waged successfully."[40]

Bloch argued that the propertied classes were "inclined to confuse even the intellectual movement against militarism with aspirations for the subversion of social order."[41] The rich failed to understand that the constant increase in the size of armies made more probable a war that would end the established (dynastic) social order.[42] The future of war, then, is "not fighting, but famine, not the slaying of men, but the bankruptcy of nations and the break-up of the whole social organization."[43]

The major threat to the established order came from government leaders' own policy of militarism. Militarism, as it existed

---

[39]See Bloch's outline of the economic consequences of war on the home front in "Opinion by Ivan S. Bliokh, Councillor of State," in *Documents Relating to the Programme of the First Hague Peace Conference* (London: Oxford at the Clarendon Press, 1921), 18–20.

[40]Bloch, "The Transvaal War, part 2," 1441; see also Bloch, *The Work of the Peace Societies*, 49–55; and Bloch, "The Transvaal War, part 1," 1318–1319.

[41]Bloch, *The Future of War*, lxvii.

[42]Adolph G. Rosengarten Jr., "John Bloch—A Neglected Prophet," *Military Review* 37 (April 1957): 34–35.

[43]Bloch, *The Future of War*, xvi–xvii; Bloch, "The Transvaal War, part 1," 1316.

then on the European continent, was based on the assumption that a regime required its army to preserve its existence against internal enemies. The necessity of a national army supposedly increased with the spread of anarchism and socialism. Bloch doubted that the army could calm the public. Rather he saw the policy of militarism increasing the effectiveness of rising socialist and anarchist agitation.[44] Starvation and deprivation made these movements revolutionary, as socialist agitators linked the existing political order and economic privation to militarism.[45] Socialist agitators, for example, claimed that armies and navies were supported by direct taxes on such necessities of life as bread and salt. Therefore, the poor took on the major economic burden of national defense and of their own oppression. While militarism provided the revolutionaries with an object to attack, "in reality," Bloch declared, "these agitators strive . . . for the destruction of the whole social order."[46] Socialist agitators were familiar with Bloch; a copy of *The Future of War* was in Lenin's Kremlin reference library,[47] and Russian revolutionaries tried to extract tactical lessons from *The Future of War* for combat against Czarist troops.[48]

Bloch predicted that the first few months of a European war would result in 500,000 deaths.[49] This prediction was borne out

[44]Bloch, *The Future of War*, lxviii.

[45]Ibid., lxii.

[46]Ibid., lxviii.

[47]Andrzej Werner, "Book Review: Jan Bloch (1836–1902): Szkic Do Portretu 'Krola Polskich Kolei,'" *International Journal of World Peace* 3 (1986): 126; *Soviet Military Encyclopedia*, 2nd ed., vol. 1 (Moscow: Military Publishing House, 1990), 416.

[48]W. Bruce Lincoln, *In War's Dark Shadow: The Russians before the Great War* (New York: Oxford University Press, 1983), 307.

[49]George Herbert Perris, *Jean de Bloch, and the Museum of War and Peace at Lucerne* (London: International Arbitration Association, 1902), 25. Bloch also cites General Rohne and General Müller, who calculated that a war fought in the open between the armies of the Triple Alliance against France and Russia would result in 11 million casualties. See Bloch, "The Wars of the Future," 319–320.

quickly. French officers led attacks for six weeks in August and September 1914 against the type of defensive positions Bloch predicted, with the result of 385,000 casualties, of which 100,000 were deaths. It took several hard years of fighting for Europe's generals to learn about the folly of frontal assaults, and it was not an easy lesson. The failure of the spring 1917 Nivelle offensive resulted in the demoralization of the French Army, with the open mutiny of sixteen separate army corps.[50] The aftermath of the war, as Bloch predicted, included major economic dislocations and the downfall of Central Europe's dynastic monarchies.

Bloch's Military Contemporaries

As Christopher Bellamy noted, Bloch was not alone in his attention to the effects of modern weaponry.[51] Toward the end of the nineteenth century, military thinkers published works that suggest they had independently arrived at conclusions similar to Bloch's—that new weapons were more efficient and destructive.[52] Indeed, the American Civil War offered military analysts appropriate evidence to infer the results of a fire-swept zone.[53] It is interesting that Bloch refers to an unnamed general who forbade his subordinates from reading published accounts of the Civil War.[54] Here is a stark example of a general who thought with a "closed set of variables"—a man who would not question or examine his dearly held assumptions.

---

[50]See Winston S. Churchill, *The World Crisis* (New York: Scribner's, 1931), 568; Leon Wolff, *In Flanders Fields: The 1917 Campaign* (New York: Time, 1958), 96–101.

[51]Bellamy, "'Civilian Experts' and Russian Defense Thinking."

[52]For example, G. F. R. Henderson, *The Science of War: A Collection of Essays and Lectures, 1892–1903* (London: Longmans, Green, 1933), 372–375.

[53]Basil Liddell Hart, *The British Way in Warfare* (London: Faber and Faber, 1932), 123.

[54]Bloch, "The Wars of the Future," 313.

Jay Luvaas determined that nearly every European analyst who argued that new and important tactical factors were evident in the American Civil War was either a junior officer or an apostate from classic military orthodoxy.[55] Senior military and civilian officials did not share Bloch's insight that tactics, strategy, acquisition policy, and doctrine would have to change, nor did they realize that analytic organizations should be created to deal with these matters.[56] Of course, these intellectual failures affected military leadership on both sides of the Atlantic. American military leaders understood that technological advances were transforming the tactics and operations of war. In 1879, for example, Chief of Staff William T. Sherman wrote: "Modern war calls for a larger measure of intelligence on the part of the individual officer and soldier than it did twenty years ago. . . . Tactical changes are forced on us, . . . thus necessitating more study and preparation on the part of the professional soldier, than in former times."[57]

During the 1880s and 1890s, the U.S. Army abandoned previously held inflexible linear tactics, tedious drill, and the stifling of individual initiative as ways to cope with what Americans called "the danger zone" and what Bloch called the "fire-swept zone." American military leaders understood that improved firepower, and especially the rate and accuracy of individual arms, but also metallic cartridges, breech-loading can-

[55]Jay Luvaas, *The Military Legacy of the Civil War: The European Inheritance* (Lawrence: University Press of Kansas, 1988).

[56]T. H. E. Travers, "Technology, Tactics, and Morale: Jean de Bloch, the Boer War, and British Military Theory, 1900–1914," *Journal of Modern History* 51 (1979): 276, 284–285. In an essay written in 1903, Henderson complained that the British army had no institutional means to collect and analyze battlefield experience. In his words, "Experience was regarded as the private property of individuals, not as a public asset, to be applied to the benefit of the army as a whole." *The Science of War*, 418–419. See also Travers, *The Killing Ground* (London: Allen and Unwin, 1987).

[57]Perry D. Jamieson, *Crossing the Deadly Ground: United States Army Tactics, 1865–1899* (Tuscaloosa: University of Alabama Press, 1994), 62.

non, and smokeless powder, made frontal assaults against entrenched defenders suicidal.[58] Lt. Gen. Philip H. Sheridan, in his November 1884 *Annual Report of the Lt. Gen. of the Army*, predicted combat operations much along the lines of World War I's western front. Sheridan said: "Armies will then resort to the spade, the pick, and the shovel; both sides will cover themselves by intrenchments, and any troops daring to make exposed attacks will be annihilated."[59] While American military leaders understood the tactical impact of technological changes, they did not draw out the broader operational and social implications of new military technologies.

In late-nineteenth-century Europe, prominent military theorists had concluded that new weapons were more efficient and destructive. Many battles in the years after the Napoleonic Wars demonstrated that, even before the modern machine gun, the massed frontal attack upon a dug-in and fairly determined defender resulted almost invariably in massive but useless casualties for the attacker.[60] Bloch cited the work of G. F. R. Henderson, who, observing British military operations in the Boer War, concluded that small-bore, quick-firing rifles and smokeless powder had revolutionized warfare.[61]

Many military theorists and generals, however, did not accept the implications of Bloch's argument at other levels of

---

[58]See for example Lt. Col. Henry M. Lazelle, "Important Improvements in the Art of War during the Past Twenty Years and Their Probable Effect on Future Military Operations," *Journal of the Military Service Institution of the United States* 3 (1882): 307–373; Capt. Francis V. Greene, "The Important Improvements in the Art of War during the Past Twenty Years and Their Probable Effect on Future Military Operations," *Journal of the Military Service Institution of the United States* 4 (1883), 1–54.

[59]Jamieson, *Crossing the Deadly Ground*, 84.

[60]Bernard Brodie, *Strategy in the Missile Age* (Princeton, NJ: Princeton University Press, 1959), 50; Athos, "Defense against Mass Attacks," *Journal of the Royal United Service Institution* 98 (February 1953), 76–81.

[61]Bloch, "The Wars of the Future," 323; see also Thomas Pakenham's statement of the Boer War's central tactical lesson, *The Boer War* (New York: Random House, 1979), 610.

analysis.[62] For example, Ardant du Picq (who died of wounds suffered while leading his regiment into its initial engagement of the Franco-Prussian War near Metz in August 1870) insisted that war does not become deadlier with the improvement of weapons—despite his familiarity with the weapons used in the American Civil War.[63] Hans Delbrück rejected Bloch's central thesis. He regarded Bloch as a dilettante and argued that Bloch's lack of military experience invalidated the work because the analysis included all sorts of improper assumptions no experienced military man would make.[64]

In published reviews of *The Future of War*, the Chief of Staff of the Russian Military District of Warsaw, Gen. Aleksander Kazimirovich Puzyrevski, criticized Bloch's "tendentious" argument, and commander of the Military District of Kiev, Gen. Mikhail Ivanovich Dragomirov, sarcastically rejected Bloch's dismissal of the role of bayonets and frontal charges in combat.[65] Many of the professional military critiques of Bloch's work emphasized that morale could overcome modern arms. In 1910 Lt. Gen. Ian Hamilton wrote:

> Blindness to moral forces and worship of material forces inevitably lead in war to destruction. All that exaggerated reliance placed upon chassepots and mitrailleuses by France before '70; all that trash written by M[onsieur] Bloch before 1904

---

[62]Travers, "Technology, Tactics, and Morale," 276, 284–285; Travers, *The Killing Ground*.

[63]Ardant du Picq, *Battle Studies: Ancient and Modern Battle* (Harrisburg, PA: Military Service Publishing, 1947), 118–131. Du Picq was responding to arguments about the tactical impact of new weapons technologies, not to Bloch specifically.

[64]Arden Bucholz, *Hans Delbrück and the German Military Establishment: War Images in Conflict* (Iowa City: University of Iowa Press, 1985), 73–75; Roger Chickering, *Imperial Germany and a World without War: The Peace Movement and German Society, 1892–1914* (Princeton, NJ: Princeton University Press, 1975), 389–390.

[65]Bellamy, "'Civilian Experts' and Russian Defense Thinking," 52; see also Bloch's comments about Dragomirov in *The Future of War*, xiv.

about zones of fire across which no living being could pass, heralded nothing but disaster. War is essentially the triumph, not of a chassepot over a needle-gun, not of a line of men entrenched behind wire entanglements and fire-swept zones over men exposing themselves in the open, but of one will over another weaker will.[66]

Writing in 1929, Maj. Gen. Sir F. Maurice tried to refute the perception that Bloch had correctly predicted the principal features of the Great War. However, Maurice misinterpreted Bloch's analysis by focusing on predictions that were not central to his thesis (e.g., the role of shrapnel shells in artillery barrages or the capability of fortresses to block advancing troops).[67]

American and European military leaders were not stupid. Yet the organization of nineteenth-century military institutions and the management style of those institutions permitted only limited trial-and-error learning. The people in military organizations could not create and aggregate knowledge systematically. Consider the intellectual challenge facing senior military leaders and nonmilitary analysts, such as Bloch, at the time. They might have recognized one or more tactical or operational problems created by new weapons technologies, but were the effects of those problems serious? What means did senior military leaders have to figure out a response to new conditions or rapid changes? What organizations and interorganizational relationships would foster testing, experimentation, and learning? How should the overall organization "learn"? What evidence would justify new acquisition policies or changes to operational

---

[66]Gen. Sir Ian Hamilton, *Compulsory Service: A Study of the Question in the Light of Experience* (London: John Murray, 1910), 121–122.

[67]Maj. Gen. Sir F. Maurice, *British Strategy: A Study of the Application of the Principles of War* (London: Constable, 1920), 10–13. See also Maurice's comments summarizing discussion of Bloch's ideas at RUSI. Bloch, "The Transvaal War, part 2," 1446–1451.

concepts and tactics? How should that evidence be created and evaluated?[68]

Where Bloch eagerly commissioned experiments to test hypotheses about weaponry and tactics, his military counterparts hesitated. Indeed, it is not clear how much would have been learned from experiments sponsored by continental military leadership. For example, Katzenbach noted that the German military, in the years prior to World War I, greatly underestimated the battlefield impact of machine guns primarily because senior officials failed to evaluate their tactics critically or to scrutinize premises and assumptions. The institutional context—the monarchy—was a key factor in the failure of military professionals to evaluate the machine gun. It seems that Emperor William II so loved the cavalry charge that war games were distorted so that the cavalry would always win. For example, observing the 1903 maneuvers, Lt. Frank R. McCoy, a young U.S. cavalry officer, was appalled by the total lack of realism in cavalry charges against artillery and rifle: "the Germans had not had the illuminating experience that the modern rifle shoots into one."[69] In 1904 Col. Alexander Godley, commander of the British mounted infantry school at Aldershot, attended the German army maneuvers in Mecklenburg-Schwerin. He noted,

> After witnessing various phases of the [landing] operations, we then proceeded along the coast towards the scene of the final manoeuvres, in which the Kaiser himself was to take part. . . . We were not much impressed. On the first of the last three days, when the two opposing army corps came to grips, there was little attempt at manoeuvre or concealment. Attacks

---

[68]See Mark D. Mandeles, "Review Essay," *Periodical: Journal of America's Military Past* 24 (Spring 1997): 67–76.

[69]Frank R. McCoy, "Notes on the German Maneuvers," *Journal of the U.S. Cavalry Association* 14 (July 1903): 27.

were made in massed formations. On one day the Kaiser commanded one side, on the next the other, and in each case his
side had the best of it. On the last day, the Kaiser put himself
at the head of the cavalry division, and on a white horse, and
followed by a huge staff, charged serried masses of infantry
and guns and put them to utter rout! The great lesson was that
there could never be any question but that the attack must
succeed.[70]

German military professionals closed the set of variables appropriate to analysis of tactical problems, and government institutions did not exist that could offer—and evaluate—competing
ideas.[71] As historian I. B. Holley showed, British and American
military organizations were neither more open to ideas nor organized to conduct rigorous analysis of ideas well.[72]

Levels of Analysis

Bellamy argued that Bloch's analysis was in substantial agreement with military professionals about the military-technical
aspects of a future European war. But Bellamy, unlike Sir Michael Howard, misinterpreted the scale, scope, and methodological implications of Bloch's work. Chief among these
implications was Bloch's realization that the complex phenomena of warfare must be approached from multiple levels of analysis and the results of these separate investigations should be
integrated. Bloch realized that methodological "scaling" problems would arise as armies grew. Actions and performances of
large armies with modern weapons were not directly propor-

---

[70]Gen. Sir Alexander Godley, *Life of an Irish Soldier* (New York: E. P. Dutton, 1939),
108.

[71]Katzenbach, "The Horse Cavalry in the Twentieth Century," 411.

[72]I. B. Holley Jr., *Ideas and Weapons* (Washington, DC: GPO, 1983).

tional to those of small armies with less advanced technology.
Indeed, Bloch also understood that it was necessary to view
warfare from several levels because entirely new social and political properties appear at each level of analysis.[73] His lecture
to the Royal United Service Institution (RUSI) began with the
following remarkable passage:

> The technical changes in the mechanism of war are accessible
> to each in his private sphere. But each expert is confined to
> his own sphere; and since every effort is made to keep secret
> the results obtained, only exceptional minds can embrace the
> whole subject, and appreciate the results of the new condi-
> tions. In addition, it must be said that the great majority of
> soldiers are strangers to the economic questions involved in
> war, while diplomatists and the chiefs of political parties have
> not the time to occupy themselves with such questions. . . .
> Absorbed in their immediate duties, very few attain a height
> of view sufficient to see all those dangers of the future.[74]

In answering his RUSI critics, Bloch lamented,

> How difficult it is to find anyone who will take a comprehen-
> sive view of the whole subject of war, not merely in regard to
> the co-relationship of the various arms, in the strictest sense
> of the word, but also in relation to those financial and eco-
> nomic resources, without the continuation of war long
> enough to obtain results would be impossible. . . . Nowhere
> do we find any clear notions of what war is as a social phe-
> nomenon, or even in the *ensemble* [sic] of its details. But war
> is not merely a series of military operations, but a great social

---

[73]Discussion of levels of analysis is a rich subject in philosophy of science and methodology. A review of the literature is not necessary here. Physics Nobel laureate
Philip W. Anderson's statement on the topic is admirably short and quite clear. See
Anderson, "More is Different," *Science* 177 (4 August 1972): 393.
[74]Bloch, "The Transvaal War, part 1," 1317.

appearance which has its ramifications in every branch of life.[75]

Bloch's multilevel approach to warfare confounded many of his critics, who essentially argued that any falsified prediction invalidates the entire theory. Given the large number of hypotheses developed by Bloch, it is not surprising that some of these were falsified. Nevertheless, modern social science methodologists and philosophers of science reject the naive elimination of the entire approach due to a few falsifications. For example, sociologist Arthur Stinchcombe contended that confusion over levels of analysis has led some analysts to believe they have refuted some theories or claims when they have not.[76] Philosopher of science Sir Karl R. Popper argued that "increase of content"—new problems, new perspectives, and new knowledge—rather than falsifiability, is a better measure of a theory's value (although falsifiability remains an important factor in the evaluation of a theory).[77] Bloch surely met this test, as his approach identified new problems and new perspectives, e.g., the analytical need to integrate the impact of higher technological performance with operational concerns for logistics, transportation, and the organization of means of production.

Warfare in the Twenty-First Century

One hundred years later, how can today's analysts learn from Jean de Bloch and develop a multilevel analytical "Bloch approach" to future warfare? They should begin by understanding the main features of warfare in the early twenty-first

---

[75]Bloch, "The Transvaal War, part 2," 1444.

[76]Arthur L. Stinchcombe, *Constructing Social Theories* (New York: Harcourt, Brace and World, 1968), 47–53.

[77]Sir Karl R. Popper, *Unended Quest* (LaSalle, IL: Open Court Publishing, 1976), 42.

century by making three key assumptions about future technology and operations: (1) new technology and operational
concepts similar to the U.S. Navy's "network-centric warfare"
will be implemented over the next ten years, (2) extensive progress in nanotechnology, robotics, and biological engineering
will be applied to manifold military systems,[78] and (3) the types
of computers, sensors, and communications systems used during the Gulf War against Iraq will continue to be improved.

Together these assumptions recognize that technological
and operational advances depend upon interrelated developments in myriad technologies and scientific domains.[79] Whether
the advance began as a response to a civilian or military problem is immaterial. The outcomes of civilian or military invention frequently affect and reinforce each other, and arguing
about the primacy of one or another pathway for subsequent
generations of inventions is unnecessary. For example, the invention of machines to bore the barrels of cast-metal cannon in
the Netherlands (in 1747) and in Great Britain (by John Wilkin-

---

[78]Recent discoveries have identified the physical limits of miniaturization of silicon
dioxide microchips: the layer of SiO_2 must be four to five atoms thick. Engineers
anticipate that this size will be achieved in the year 2012. (Max Schulz, "The End of
the Road for Silicon?" *Nature* 399 [24 June 1999]: 729–730.) Complementary research has forged layers of individual molecules into devices called "chemically assembled electronic nanocomputers," machines that would be billions of times more
powerful than today's computers. There is a great deal of interesting and powerful
research on these topics. For example, see Robert F. Service, "Organic Molecule Re-
wires Chip Design," *Science* 285 (16 July 1999): 313–314; C. P. Collier, et al., "Electronically Configurable Molecular-Based Logic Gates," *Science* 285 (16 July 1999):
391–393; Philip G. Collins and Phaedon Avouris, "Nanotubes for Electronics," *Scientific American* 278 (December 2000): 62–69; John Markoff, "Scientists, Using New
Material, Push Toward Tinier Computers," *New York Times*, 27 April 2001, www
.nytimes.com/2001/04/27/technology/27CHIP.htm/; Kenneth Chang, "I.B.M. Creates a Tiny Circuit Out of Carbon," *New York Times*, 27 August 2001. Progress in
the design of quantum computers may avoid the physical limits on computer design
imposed by silicon. Anne Eisenberg, "What's Next: Quantum Theory Could Ex-
pand the Limits of Computer Chips," *New York Times*, 20 September 2001.
[79]See for example Henry Petroski, *The Pencil: A History of Design and Circumstance*
(New York: Alfred A. Knopf, 1992).

son in 1775) made possible the creation of the steam engine. Inventing the steam engine in 1765, James Watt formulated the idea for a separate condenser (to keep the cylinder hot). Construction of the engine was delayed by the lack of the ability to bore a very precise cylinder that would prevent the escape of steam between its walls and the piston, but in 1776 Watt's first two engines were finally set to work.[80] The military then applied steam-engine technology to a variety of tasks, including transportation and in the process created a new set of opportunities and problems in the exercise of command, mobility, and so on.

One can't predict the occurrence or impact of technology that has not yet been invented. However, one can identify policy trade-offs, conflicts, and implications that derive from the interaction of factors at different levels of analysis. Following Bloch's example, we may examine future warfare from three levels of analysis relevant to today: (1) military technology; (2) information, knowledge, and analysis requirements for individual decision making; and (3) the structure of combat organization. The combination of these levels of analysis illuminates how the application to combat of new or evolving technologies creates new opportunities or problems for people using the technologies and for the organizations in which the people and machines operate.[81]

In addition, as Bloch's work demonstrated, new technology also demands appropriate advances in social structure—the educational and intellectual skills, roles, and norms of behavior—

---

[80]T. K. Derry and Trevor I. Williams, *A Short History of Technology: From Earliest Times to A.D. 1900* (New York: Oxford University Press, 1961), 150, 321–322, 350.

[81]The examination of these three levels of analysis assumes an institutional context provided by the U.S. Constitution and the interplay of executive and legislative branches of government and of various nongovernmental organizations. The examination of future warfare options for another country, such as the People's Republic of China, would have to address the impact of institutions on the other levels of analysis.

that allow people to use the technology to best advantage. Many weapons or tools wait years for an appropriate social structure to emerge to make employment feasible.[82] The crossbow, for example, was invented fifteen hundred years before it saw wide use. The absence of an appropriate social structure limited its employment, but the rise of the castle made the crossbow an integral part of a violent and elitist social revolution. A short description of the crossbow's history illustrates this issue:

> Fortifications in pre-Norman times were often fairly simple affairs, designed for use and intended to shelter the entire population of an area. Thus there would be plenty of firepower inside the walls when the inhabitants took refuge against a marauding band. The Normans imposed control through a small, heavily armed military minority that dominated the much larger peasant and town populations. Their castles were intended to shelter the few from the many as well as from armed and predatory members of their own caste. The superior range of the crossbow helped them to secure these refuges.[83]

In our time, the widespread distribution of "information" and computer technologies and the training in their use make entirely new military roles and operational concepts possible. It is hard to imagine the capability to design, operate, and innovate the use of advanced command, control, communication, computer, intelligence, surveillance, and reconnaissance (C⁴ISR) equipment and software by personnel whose educational background consists of memorization of religious doctrine, as in Saudi Arabia.[84]

---

[82] Arthur L. Stinchcombe, "Social Structure and Organizations," in *Handbook of Organizations*, ed. James G. March (Chicago: Rand McNally, 1965), 1422–1423.

[83] Vernard Foley, George Palmer, and Werner Soedel, "The Crossbow," *Scientific American* 252 (January 1985): 104.

[84] Howard Schneider, "Rote Schooling in Saudi Arabia Leaves Students Ill-Suited to Work," *Washington Post*, 12 June 1999, A13.

The next chapter will follow the methodology of tracing policy, organizational decision making, and technology trade-offs by examining the assumptions underlying command and control (C^2) arrangements in the context of the Gulf War air campaign.

Chapter 4

Command and Control at the Dawn of a Military Revolution

The new image of the military of the twenty first century is a totally integrated, electronically linked, fully computerized fighting force, trained for and fighting on an electronic battlefield. . . . Such tight control goes against the lesson that confusion and disorder . . . will remain the natural state of combat, however advanced, sophisticated, and precise the new systems might appear to be when tested in peace-time.[1]

To achieve the digitized ideal of the twenty-first-century military much of the effort to design the future military must focus on command and control (C²) architectures. The challenge is to arrange the flow of information and instructions to improve the intelligence and rationality of decision making. The goal is to optimize the calculation of options and the execution of actions in uncertain and complex choice situations.[2]

Measured by the acquisition of ever more computers and communications equipment and the number of administrative reorganizations carried out each year, the results of efforts to improve C² have been mixed—and largely disappointing. Na-

---

[1]Gene I. Rochlin, *Trapped in the Net: The Unanticipated Consequences of Computerization* (Princeton, NJ: Princeton University Press, 1997), 207.

[2]Thomas P. Coakley, *Command and Control for War and Peace* (Washington, DC: NDU Press, 1992), 75.

tional security analyst Samuel P. Huntington notes that the same organizational deficiencies have been noted in "every significant study of the Defense Department, official or unofficial, since the 1950s."[3] Indeed, the aggregated residue of many previous reforms at levels ranging from the tactical unit to the theater command structure distorted C^2 relationships in Operation Desert Storm in the Persian Gulf.[4] As then–Air Force Chief of Staff Gen. Merrill A. McPeak stated: "We don't know whether the command structure was really tough enough, durable enough, to really survive difficult combat conditions. Unhappily, complex and confusing command arrangements exist not only in situations like Desert Storm but are also a feature of our day-to-day existence."[5] The administrative objects of General McPeak's concern—decision making, coordination, communication, hierarchy, and effective action—are central and long-standing problems of command.

While many factors affect the performance of C^2, the key challenge facing U.S. C^2 is the way individual-level and organizational-level activities and reforms intersect. This "levels of analysis" problem is the main focus of this chapter, which

[3]Samuel P. Huntington, "Centralization of Authority in Defense Organizations," in C^3I: Issues of Command and Control, ed. Thomas P. Coakley (Washington, DC: NDU Press, 1985), 225. James Q. Wilson adds that reorganizations fail to affect the behavior of the targeted organization in part because they proceed without consideration of what people do. Wilson, Bureaucracy: What Government Agencies Do and Why They Do It (New York: Basic Books, 1989), 11–12, Page 380n.25 lists several studies which describe how reorganizations fail, but omits Herbert A. Simon, "Applying Information Technology to Organization Design," Public Administration Review 33 (1973): 268–278.

[4]Coakley describes how individual reforms can distort the process of C^2 over time. He notes that the "complexity and dynamics of C^2 frustrate rationalistic attempts to fix or improve pieces of the process. One isolated fix—a highly capable new radio, for example—spawns another problem, in the case of the new radio, another 'interface' problem." Coakley, Command and Control for War and Peace, 181.

[5]Tony Capaccio, "USAF Chief Plans War's Command Chain," Defense News (2 December 1991): 1.

draws primary examples from U.S. experiences during the Gulf War air campaign.[6] Although the Gulf War took place more than ten years ago, the continued development and automation of C⁴ISR equipment do not change the conceptual issues involved in the design of C^2 organization and procedures.

This section will examine C^2 organization by describing assumptions underlying efforts to improve the intelligence of military organizations. Three factors shape the analysis: First, U.S. force structure is shrinking and will continue to decrease in the post–Cold War era. Second, improved C^2 has been, and will continue to be, the basis of doing more with less.[7] And third, in war, what matters is a competitive advantage over the enemy—not perfection. Armies win wars not because they are perfect but because they fight other armies less well commanded, trained, or equipped. The goal of defense analysis should be to improve competitive advantage rather than to propose a technically perfect set of war-fighting information and communications technologies. Each advance in understanding C^2 puts the U.S. military in a more effective posture to employ the strengths and mitigate the weaknesses of our own forces and to exploit the vulnerabilities of our adversaries.

---

[6]C^2 deficiencies have many causes, including inadequate personnel or equipment, poor military doctrine, the size of the forces being commanded, inappropriate architecture (e.g., the number of people and components in headquarters' staff, specification of routines and rules, and information flows within and between units and components), or the bad luck of pitting an organization designed for one type of conflict (e.g., conventional warfare in Europe) into a novel or unexpected situation (e.g., guerrilla warfare in Southeast Asia).

[7]In the 1980s defense analysts began to argue that "the next war will be won not by the side with the most tanks and aircraft but the side with the fastest, most redundant, most reliable, and most survivable C³I [command, control, communications, and intelligence] systems." D. G. Meyer, "DOD Likely to Spend $250 Billion on C3I through 1990," *Armed Forces Journal International* (February 1985): 73; see also Coakley, *Command and Control for War and Peace*, 177; N. Munro, "Simulation Proves Battlefield Value of C³," *Defense News* (2 August 1993): 18, 20.

Problems of C^2

Since the beginning of organized warfare, the central problem of military forces' C^2 has been an intellectual problem of organizing—and then gaining access to—information, knowledge, and understanding. Although leadership—namely, the ability to motivate people to put their lives at risk for others—is important, for analytic and pragmatic reasons, it is critical to separate concerns relating to personality characteristics and charisma from those relating to special properties and relationships of formal organizations that are independent of individuals. We cannot teach people how to have charisma, but we can learn how to devise more effective procedures and organizations.

Organizing the flow of information and knowledge is a problem, as military historian Martin van Creveld argues, of achieving certainty concerning all factors that bear on the application of military force. Over time, military and nonmilitary technologies and the size of combatant forces have altered and modified the equipment and tactics of C^2. Eighteenth- and nineteenth-century armies, for example, were larger than their predecessors; this increase in army size was made possible by improved administrative techniques. However, information transmission technology, upon which C^2 depended, had not undergone a similar improvement. The technical and operational difficulties in transmitting appropriate and timely information and orders within those armies during combat made it difficult to take full advantage of their size and resulting firepower. Therefore, military theorists coped with their information transmission problem—and the resulting imperfect information and uncertainty—by proposing tactical- and strategic-level solutions. In effect, eighteenth- and nineteenth-century military theorists accepted and implemented modern ideas about bounded rationality: not everything can be known; decisions are based on incomplete information about alternatives and their consequences; and gathering and organizing information is costly.

Tactically, the solution to the errors inherent in transmitting information and instructions lay in imposition of discipline and routines—as practiced in drill, which allowed relatively large portions of a battle to be programmed. Drill, revived from Greek and Roman armies, was a sixteenth-century tactical innovation to make employment of new weapons technologies more effective.[8] The programming of routine through drill was critical for at least four reasons: (1) the relative complexity of weapons facilitated greater opportunity for error (e.g., double loading a musket or forgetting to withdraw a ramrod), (2) the precise array of troops allowed the concentration of greatest firepower and the prevention of accidents, (3) the unreliability and slow rate of musket fire made coordinated employment of muskets necessary to ensure that at least some barrels would be loaded and ready to fire at any given moment, and (4) the cooperation of musketeers with pikemen demanded complex evolutions, such as the repeated opening and closing of ranks.[9]

Strategically, military theorists began to experiment with span of control and hierarchy. Beginning around 1760, French military leaders divided armies into self-contained permanent strategic units (hence the term, "divisions"). Each unit was made up of a combination of all arms, its own headquarters, and a system of communications. As a result, first the division, then the corps, and finally the general staff appeared to coordinate the movement of the army as a whole. Commanders found that being able to operate armies dispersed over a larger geographic

---

[8]Harald Kleinschmidt, "Using the Gun: Manual Drill and the Proliferation of Portable Firearms," *The Journal of Military History* 63 (July 1999): 601–630.

[9]See Jacob de Gheyn, *The Exercise of Armes: A Seventeenth Century Military Manual* (London: Greenhill Books, 1986); Martin van Creveld, *Technology and War: From 2000 B.C. to the Present* (New York: Free Press, 1989), 92–93.

area greatly increased the number of strategic combinations available. The set-piece battle, in which commanders exercised continuous and direct control over their forces, began to decline because control of such large and dispersed forces was very difficult. The increased difficulty of determining an adversary's intentions further complicated a commander's understanding of the combat environment and, as a result, the number of encounter battles increased after 1790.[10]

The tactical and strategic solutions to the problems of information transmission, ambiguity, and uncertainty created new problems for military theorists, commanders, and heads of state. On the strategic level, the division of larger armies into self-contained units increased the commander's coordination problems among those units. Not surprisingly, how military leaders organized to collect, analyze and process, and disseminate information and orders is a central topic in military history and is a focus of debates about the success and failure of military campaigns and their leaders.

Today, the increased lethality and mobility of military forces places greater demands than ever before upon the C^2 system—equipment, people, and organizations. The size and complexity of the intellectual task of C^2 facing today's military commanders would have overwhelmed the "Great Captains" of earlier times as would have the accuracy, mobility, and lethality of today's weapons systems. Indeed, many defense analysts have noted that the systems employed by the United States against Iraq provided a "revolutionary advance in military capability. . . . An army with such technology [intelligence sensors, defense suppression systems, and precision guidance subsystems] has an overwhelming advantage over an army without it."[11] Yet, advances in such weapons and military-support tech-

---

[10]Van Creveld, *Technology and War*, 120–122.
[11]William J. Perry, "Desert Storm and Deterrence," *Foreign Affairs* 70 (1991): 66.

nology are outpacing the ability of available C² organization to employ and control them. Two measures of this phenomenon are the increasingly significant problems of "friendly fire" (i.e., the infliction of casualties upon one's own troops) and of information overload.[12]

Models of Decision Making: Individual. The design of previous C² organizational reforms has been guided by the unexamined assumption that intelligent-individual-decision-making procedures are an appropriate model for organizational decisions. As Carl H. Builder notes, although personalities and conflicting interests intrude, the logic of this decision-making model "is assiduously maintained" in the Army, Navy, Air Force, and Marine Corps.[13] The model is well known and has four basic steps: (1) define one's goal(s), (2) list all options to achieve the goal(s), (3) evaluate each option in terms of the extent to which it can achieve the goal(s), and (4) choose the best, i.e., optimal, option.

This approach to decision making often is associated with particular organizational characteristics: clear and efficient, simple and neat, streamlined, "lean and mean." These words carry positive emotional baggage. Their converse—overlapping and inefficient, messy and fragmented, confused, bloated, and duplicative—carries negative overtones. Yet, the persuasive language used to describe and recommend the single-decision-maker model and its associated organizational properties should rouse suspicion. The object of this language is, of course, to support the argument that an "efficient" overall decision

---

[12]Adm. J. W. Prueher, "Information Age Overload," *Defense News* 13 (30 November 1998): 23; Jeffrey T. Richelson, "Volume of Data Cripples Tactical Intelligence System," *Armed Forces Journal International* 129 (June 1992): 35–37.

[13]Carl H. Builder, *The Masks of War: American Military Styles in Strategy and Analysis* (Baltimore: Johns Hopkins University Press, 1989), 5.

process enhances organizational rationality and intelligence and, thus, the prospects for combat victory. In reality, however, as James G. March showed in civilian organizations, the policy prescriptions for organizational structure and relationships normally flowing from this perspective may actually degrade organizational rationality and intelligence.[14] The individual-decision-making model's applicability to organizational design has wide prescriptive appeal.[15] It is particularly seductive to military organizations, in which "the ideology of military decision making emphasizes the imposition of order through organization and command and the importance of clarity, coherence and comprehensiveness."[16] How appropriate is this decision model to the design of military C^2 and especially for future military organizations?

Regardless of whether it is a useful design prescription, the single-decision-maker model does not describe what happens in military organizations. Reflection on Gen. H. Norman Schwarzkopf's description of miscommunications among himself, President George H. W. Bush, Gen. Colin Powell, and the President's national security staff is instructive. During the first days after Bush declared a naval blockade against Iraq—and before the United Nations's Security Council had granted per-

---

[14]James G. March, "The Technology of Foolishness," in *Readings in Managerial Psychology*, 2nd ed., eds. H. Leavitt and L. R. Pondy (Chicago: University of Chicago Press, 1973).

[15]In the defense arena, at least since the McNamara era, rational scientific language and symbols "have gained greater popular acceptability, credibility, and use." Garry D. Brewer, "Comments on 'Producing Policy Papers,'" in *Advances in Information Processing in Organizations*, eds. Lee S. Sproull, P. D. Larkey, Robert F. Coulam, and M. A. Smith (Greenwich, CT: JAI Press, 1985), 209; see also Ida R. Hoos, *Systems Analysis in Public Policy: A Critique* (Berkeley: University of California Press, 1972), 9–10, 136–137, 241.

[16]James G. March and Roger Weissinger-Baylon, introduction to *Ambiguity and Command: Organizational Perspectives on Military Decision Making*, eds. March and Weissinger-Baylon (Boston: Pitman Publishing, 1986), 1.

mission to reinforce the embargo by military means—the President's national security staff had no prepared answer for questions of how the Navy should handle intercoastal tankers. Upon discovery of such a tanker, there ensued a tense twenty-four-hour period for Schwarzkopf and leaders in Washington of missed opportunities to communicate, misunderstandings, frequent revisions of instructions, and miscalculations.[17] Goals were poorly articulated and potential conflicts among them were unanticipated. A comprehensive list of policy options was not proposed, nor was each option evaluated in the context of its impact on an evolving set of goals.

The critical question for C² organizational design is not whether different perspectives on immediate tactical problems exist between national and theater operational authority. We know these perspectives have frequently been quite different. Instead, we should note that despite years of administrative tinkering to create clean and streamlined decision making—in accordance with assumptions of intelligent individual decision making—the outcomes of such organizational arrangements continue to frustrate the C² designers' intentions.

Models of Decision Making: Organizational. Thinking about organizational behavior solely in terms of choices made by senior leaders introduces systematic bias into interpretations of decision processes. The fundamental presumption of virtually all decision-making models and theories is that decision processes are organized around the act of making decisions and are understandable in terms of decision outcomes.[18] In this ideal vi-

---

[17]H. Norman Schwarzkopf with Peter Petre, *It Doesn't Take a Hero* (New York: Bantam Books, 1992), 321-322.

[18]Martin Landau and Paul Schulman, "Political Science and Public Policy" (paper prepared for delivery at the 1984 annual meeting of the American Political Science Association, Washington, DC).

sion of decision making, information clarifies decision options. Participants in the process influence substantive decisions and interpret the activities of making decisions in terms of the decisions that are made. Yet, this ideal vision does not describe how the Gulf War's air campaign was planned or managed, and empirical research on organizations has shown that these presumptions may be misleading in at least three respects.[19]

First, most theories of choice overestimate the coherence of decision processes.[20] In military organizations, the senior leaders' explicit intentions and the coherence of choices are often lost in the movement of people, problems, and solutions within the organization. Solutions are linked to problems, and decision makers to choices, more often by happenstance than by causal relevance. Armed with retrospective knowledge of the war's outcome and the actions of key participants, historians may see a single path and an inner logic to the planning process. However, the Gulf War planning efforts of the Army, Navy, Marine Corps, and Air Force were roughly independent and parallel.

Prior to the Gulf War, the movement of people, problems, and solutions within the Air Staff illustrates how chance encounters—rather than a coherent decision process—coalesced into what came to be known as the "Instant Thunder" briefing.[21] On 10 August 1990 General Schwarzkopf called

---

[19]James G. March, *Decisions and Organizations* (New York: Basil Blackwell, 1989).

[20]Michael D. Cohen, James G. March, and Johan P. Olsen, "A Garbage Can Model of Organizational Choice," *Administrative Science Quarterly* 17 (1972): 1–17; James G. March and Johan P. Olsen, "Garbage Can Models of Decision Making in Organizations," in *Ambiguity and Command*, eds. March and Weissinger-Baylon; Karl E. Weick, "Educational Organizations as Loosely Coupled Systems," *Administrative Science Quarterly* 21 (1976): 1–19; John W. Kingdon, *Agendas, Alternatives, and Public Policies* (Boston: Little, Brown, 1984); March, *Decisions and Organizations*, 13, 390–391.

[21]The Instant Thunder briefing, now unclassified, originally was classified top secret and limited distribution. See Thomas C. Hone, Mark D. Mandeles, and Sanford S. Terry, *Gulf War Air Power Survey*, vol. 1, part 2, *Command and Control* (Washing-

General Powell to ask that Air Staff planners begin work "on a strategic bombing campaign aimed at Iraq's military," which would provide appropriate retaliatory options. Schwarzkopf asked for Air Staff planning help because his component staff, organizationally responsible for developing a broad plan for combat, was too busy facilitating the deployment of aircraft to Saudi Arabia and planning to blunt a potential Iraqi attack on that country.[22]

The Instant Thunder briefing, built primarily by prophet of airpower Col. John A. Warden III and Lt. Col. David A. Deptula, set the basic agenda for the planning and conduct of the war. In early August 1990 neither Warden nor Deptula worked for a combat command or on the Joint Staff, the organizations that formally handle war planning. Warden and Deptula happened to be in the right place (the Air Staff) at the right time (August 1990) to apply the airpower perspective (their preferred solution) to the initial task of designing a response to a potential Iraqi invasion of Saudi Arabia (the problem). Warden's Air Staff office, called "Checkmate," and the offensive planning cell in Saudi Arabia (variously known as the "Black Hole" or the guidance, apportionment, and targeting [GAT] cell) became the focal points for "collections of solutions looking for problems."[23] These "solutions" looking for "problems" were the officers' unyielding prewar beliefs concerning how to apply military aviation to combat situations.[24]

---

ton, DC: GPO, 1993). See chap. 6 for a brief overview of the initial development and evolution of this briefing.

[22]This situation was unique. If war had begun in Europe, there would have been no need to request Air Staff planning support because European Command (EUCOM) had sufficient staff to handle such an eventuality. Schwarzkopf, *It Doesn't Take a Hero*, 313–320.

[23]James G. March and Johan P. Olsen, "Organizing Political Life: What Administrative Reorganization Tells Us about Government," *American Political Science Review* 77 (June 1983): 286.

[24]Mark D. Mandeles, Thomas C. Hone, and Sanford S. Terry, *Managing "Command and Control" in the Persian Gulf War* (Westport, CT: Praeger, 1996).

In decision theory, information strategies are designed to resolve uncertainties about future states of the world that are relevant to choices faced by decision makers. Actual information processing in Saudi Arabia did not fit this characterization. For instance, after the war some GAT planners expressed surprise at the range of planning conducted behind unmarked doors down the hall or by Central Command (CENTCOM) officers working in the Saudi Ministry of Defense building a mile away. In addition, a good deal of information gathered was "compartmented" and kept within offices among only people having the appropriate clearances and "need to know." In other words, intelligence information was gathered and processed in various rooms of the Royal Saudi Air Force building with little regard for its relevance to the overall campaign. There were significant gaps in GAT or Black Hole officers' knowledge of the range of activities taking place elsewhere in the building or in the tents set up in the parking lot outside. Even when they did have access to knowledge, GAT planners, guided by their own conception of strategic air warfare, discarded or ignored information inconsistent with their views.[25]

Second, while information is used in making decisions, gathering and using information is often better understood as symbolic action. One manifestation of such symbolic action was in efforts of planners to avoid uncertainty and to reduce anxiety. For example, GAT planners used information derived from computer-based models of missions primarily as a "gut check"—that is, as a means to reduce anxiety about the outcomes of plans. In planning the air campaign during Desert Shield, computer models helped GAT campaign planners justify decisions regarding which aircraft (e.g., F-117 rather than F-16) to use to attack particular targets.[26]

---

[25]Ibid., chap. 3.

[26]Computer model output inconsistent with plans or ideas of key planners would have been ignored. Hone, Mandeles, and Terry, *Command and Control*, appendix 3.

Symbolism also plays a role in senior leaders' representations of problems and solutions. In organizations, problems search for solutions, but solutions also search for problems, for which they might be imagined to be the solution. For example, the Joint Force Air Component Commander (JFACC) concept was seen as the solution for political problems dating to the 1930s regarding the centralization of authority, assignment of roles, apportionment of missions among the military services, and mediation of disputes between airmen and soldiers. Proponents of the JFACC concept seized on the Gulf War as an opportunity to solve those long-standing political problems.[27] Organizational members cared about outcomes—e.g., defeating the Iraqis—but they also cared about the symbolic meaning of victory and the means by which victory was obtained. Although it was evident very early that the allied coalition would win the war, it became vitally important to Air Force campaign-planning officers that the victory show the decisiveness of airpower and the indispensability of the JFACC in managing airpower.[28]

Finally, the conditions under which rationality works best are relatively rare in organizations. Rationality is not an ill-conceived goal. A rational model may improve decision making when (1) the environment changes slowly, (2) stable means-ends relationships exist that are known to be effective for the type of problem at hand, (3) only a few groups try to affect decisions, and (4) agents with centralized authority control the situation.[29] However, organizational actors rarely proceed by

[27]Charles A. Horner, "The Air Campaign," *Military Review* (September 1991): 20–21. For a historical view of these problems, see Jeffery S. Underwood, *The Wings of Democracy: The Influence of Air Power on the Roosevelt Administration, 1933–1941* (College Station: Texas A&M University Press, 1991), chap. 4.

[28]Mandeles, Hone, and Terry, *Managing "Command and Control,"* chaps. 3 and 5.

[29]Numerous analyses examine how prescriptions of rational models for commanders are upset during wartime. The most celebrated is Clausewitz's discussion of "fric-

perceiving a problem, defining the problem carefully, generating possible actions solely because they might solve the stated problem, and selecting the single best way to proceed.[30]

Theories of strategic action assume that intelligent strategies for a single actor in a simple world will prove equally intelligent for a large war-fighting organization operating in a complex environment involving many actors making choices simultaneously. This analogy is flawed. When the tasks are relatively complex, intelligent action in a particular case is difficult to determine.[31] Indeed, many initially attractive strategies will prove to be less attractive with deeper analysis or longer experience. Furthermore, individual decision making is much different from an organizational decision process wherein individuals work together. Air campaign planning decision problems, for example, have greater complexity, variety, and impact than those that can be comprehended by a single individual. Campaign decision problems involve coordinating many people within a hierarchical organization and with other people in similarly structured organizations. This observation has important

---

tion." In Clausewitz's words, "Everything in war is very simple, but the simplest thing is difficult. The difficulties accumulate and end by producing a kind of friction that is inconceivable unless one has experienced war." Carl von Clausewitz, in *On War*, eds. and trans. Michael Howard and Peter Paret (Princeton, NJ: Princeton University Press, 1984), 119–21.

[30]This generalization refers to decision making within organizations, e.g., in planning staffs, where multiple (and partially conflicting) goals may coexist, tasks may change quickly, problems faced by the staff may change quickly, many persons are involved in the decision making, and some causal knowledge may be applied to achieve desired ends. A significant exception to this generalization is in the training company-level ground officers receive. While it is acknowledged (by trainers during the training process) that the initial plan may change, the company leader is taught to approach each tactical problem by defining a goal, generating and comparing possible actions to achieve that goal, and choosing the most reasonable option. This approach to tactical problems structures the company leader's thinking when conditions "on the ground" differ from what he expected, and helps him modify his plan. I am indebted to Dr. David André for his insights into decision making.

[31]Jonathan B. Bendor and Thomas H. Hammond, "Rethinking Allison's Models," *American Political Science Review* 86 (June 1992): 304.

implications for the design of appropriate future military combat organizations.

Organizational Features of C^2

Formal organizations result from the establishment of explicit procedures to coordinate the activities of a group in the interest of achieving specified ends. One reason organizations form is to circumvent limits on memory and other cognitive constraints on individuals as information processors and decision makers. In this context, organizations are "machinery for coping with the limits of man's ability to comprehend and compute in the face of uncertainty."[32]

The military, like other complex formal organizations, attempts to ease the constraints on information processing and problem solving that confront individuals who do the organization's work. There is a great deal of literature about the kinds of problems that organizations may respond to less intelligently than individuals, e.g., by stifling innovations through pressures to conform or follow rules.[33] Yet, for other kinds of problems, organizations may be smarter than individuals because of (1) parallel processing of information, (2) the use of appropriate administrative redundancies, and (3) the use of standard operating procedures (SOPs) for common problems.[34] The question for the military is whether formal military organizational structure enhances intelligent decision making during wartime. The key

---

[32]Herbert A. Simon, "Rational Decision Making in Business Organizations," *American Economic Review* 68 (1979): 501; James G. March and Herbert A. Simon, *Organizations* (New York: John Wiley and Sons, 1958), 189.

[33]Irving L. Janis, *Victims of Groupthink: A Psychological Study of Foreign Policy Decisions and Fiascoes* (Boston: Houghton Mifflin, 1972).

[34]Herbert A. Simon, *Administrative Behavior* (New York: Free Press, 1957); March and Simon, *Organizations*; Bendor and Hammond, "Rethinking Allison's Models."

organizational aspects of C² relevant to this question include hierarchy, coordination, division of labor, and conflict.

Hierarchy. Commanding military forces involves comparing information, policy options, and implementation proposals. As in any organization, the shape of a military hierarchy affects who handles which issues, who makes which comparisons, and how goals and capabilities are linked. An organization's hierarchy determines the sequence of decisions, thus influencing which policies are adopted.[35] The organization's hierarchy also determines who executes and implements particular tasks. In effect, the hierarchy represents a partial anticipation of the problems to be found in the organization's environment and the solutions to those problems.

Combat commands engaged in military operations are large, highly specialized, and complex. C² relationships are predicated on achieving certainty concerning the factors that affect the application of force. Yet, the size, specialization, and complexity of the military organization inhibit attaining that certainty. For many tasks entailed by the actual planning and execution of the Desert Storm air campaign, staff abandoned the prewar understanding of how the air campaign C² organization would operate. The "intelligence" suborganization, staffed by people who identified and analyzed targets and attacks, was ignored in favor of ad hoc relationships at several organizational levels, sustained by modern communications technology that allowed discussions over great distances about classified topics. To direct attacks against mobile targets, senior planners bypassed the formal organization designed to transmit guidance for daily at-

---

[35]Bendor and Hammond, "Rethinking Allison's Models," 317; Thomas P. Hammond, "Toward a General Theory of Hierarchy: Books, Bureaucrats, Basketball Tournaments, and the Administrative Structure of the Nation-State," *Journal of Public Administration Research and Theory* 3 (1993): 120–145.

tacks to the flying squadrons. As a result, those pilots who were redirected often flew without necessary preparation or supporting aircraft. In each case, the formal hierarchy provided neither the means to make the appropriate choices, comparisons, and evaluations, nor communications channels with the required short time lags. Reviews of the 1999 Kosovo air campaign suggest that the formal organization also was unable to consistently provide timely tasking and target guidance, intelligence, and feedback about attacks' effects. Once again, an ad hoc organization had to be constructed while aircraft were flying in combat.[36]

Coordination. Forming and maintaining military (or social, economic, and political) organizations can create coordination problems. The modes of coordination—formal (through procedures) and informal (through shared doctrine or belief systems)—lead to different constraints on information flows, attention, and activity. Within an organization, the transmission and reception of information assumes the existence (and prior creation) of stylized or simplified representations of the real world. As noted above, for example, the GAT's approach to defeating Iraq was based upon a concept of strategic airpower as a complete, independent force on the battlefield, reflected in the Instant Thunder plan Air Staff officers devised in August 1990. Instant Thunder proposed that a major, if not deciding, factor in forcing a regime to surrender was precise, overwhelming aerial attack against "centers of gravity"—key people or political, industrial, economic, social, and military institutions or

[36]Michael Ignatieff, "The Virtual Commander," *The New Yorker*, 2 August 1999, 33; Michael Ignatieff, *Virtual War: Kosovo and Beyond* (New York: Metropolitan Books, 2000); Department of Defense, *Report to Congress: Kosovo/Operation Allied Force After-Action Report*, 31 January 2000.

systems.[37] The plan, in effect, asserted a causal relationship between the destruction of Iraqi centers of gravity and the continued Iraqi war effort, and thus directed air campaign planners to
choose and rank targets to attack on a twenty-four-hour basis.
Yet, internal representations, such as the unifying view presented by Instant Thunder, may be related only loosely to outside reality. (Years after the war, the causal relationship posited
between destruction of centers of gravity and Iraqi government
behavior has yet to manifest itself as in compliance with UN
Security Council resolutions.) The value of internal representations is in reducing the range and variation of potential communications and messages—i.e., to allow people to operate from
the "same page."

Division of Labor. Functional divisions of labor in an organization and the rules people learn (also known as socialization) for
conducting subunit activities or employing technologies lead to
the development of conflicting experiences, technologies, and
tasks. Subunit goals will diverge as the organization grows
larger and more complex. The organization will rely more on

---

[37]In *The Air Campaign* (Washington, DC: NDU Press, 1988), John Warden referred
to a portion of Carl von Clausewitz's definition of center of gravity (pp. 9–10).
Clausewitz employed a mechanical metaphor to analyze the relationship between adversaries (for a discussion of the role of analogies in analysis, see Martin Landau,
Political Theory and Political Science [New York: Macmillan, 1972], chap. 3). Clausewitz defined center of gravity as "the hub of all power and movement, on which
everything depends. That is the point against which all our energies should be directed." Howard and Paret, *On War*, 595–596. In addition, the official U.S. Air Force
manual on aerospace doctrine cites Clausewitz's use of center of gravity to refer to
particular relationships and people, such as (1) the capital of countries subject to domestic strife, (2) the forces of large, protective countries on small, reliant countries,
(3) the issue binding allied parties together, and (4) the personalities of the leaders of
popular uprisings. This reference to Clausewitz is included in *Air Force Manual 1-1,*
vol. 2, *Basic Aerospace Doctrine of the United States Air Force* (Washington, DC: Air
Staff, 1992), 276; see also Richard P. Hallion, *Storm over Iraq: Air Power and the Gulf
War* (Washington, DC: Smithsonian Institution Press, 1992), 116.

formal procedures to coordinate activities as functional specialization increases.[38]

Senior Gulf War air leaders pursued different goals, which varied according to their hierarchical positions, their roles, and the types of tasks they confronted. Lieutenant General Horner, for example, as JFACC, dealt with the problem of defining the JFACC. Brigadier General Glosson, as senior air campaign planner and commander of the fighter and attack aircraft division (the 14th Air Division [P]), concerned himself with the dual problems of winning the war and demonstrating the decisiveness of airpower. Senior air intelligence officers (e.g., Col. John Leonardo) wanted to demonstrate the usefulness of organizational procedures developed during peacetime to analyze and transmit intelligence information. Sometimes these different goals clashed, as in the conflict between Glosson and Leonardo over the timeliness of the intelligence information transmitted to the air campaign planners. Other times, no conflict resulted from the separate pursuit of solutions to different problems or goals: Brigadier General Glosson's goals and actions did not interfere with Lieutenant General Horner's efforts to establish precedents for future JFACCs.[39]

Functional divisions of labor may cause the overall organization to come to represent a coalition of partially conflicting interests and subunits instead of a single and coherent body with compatible and overlapping values. Cooperation, in a coalition, is the result of a continual process of bargaining and negotiation—a process that must be restarted when personnel turnover is high.

---

[38]March and Simon, *Organizations*, 144–146; John P. Crecine, "Defense Resource Allocation: Garbage Can Analysis of C³ Procurement," in *Ambiguity and Command*, eds. March and Weissinger-Baylon, 77.

[39]Mandeles, Hone, and Terry, *Managing "Command and Control,"* chap. 3.

Conflict in Organizations. Organizational decision making involves many participants, each having individual preferences (and potentially different rank ordering of those preferences). Organizational leaders will have to "smooth over" these preferences, much as politicians settle differences. The military organization fighting the war in Saudi Arabia operated under a political system in that a variety of goals and preferences ancillary to winning the war nevertheless found their way into the decision process—and these goals affected the way the war was run. Decisions about the JFACC and about C^2 were influenced by the tacit recognition that battles over the budget, roles, and missions would be fought even after the war.

Individuals and groups within an organization use their resources, including control over information, as leverage for pursuing their own interests. Self-interested manipulation of information is a constant and palpable feature of organizational life. This fact helps put into context the appearance of problems between the intelligence community in theater and the GAT.[40]

Structural features of an organization limit the ability of the most senior decision makers to deal with conflicting demands simultaneously. For example, the JFACC, Lieutenant General Horner, could not direct war fighting personally. First, scarcities of time and energy imposed limits on his attention, which was focused on current problems and goals, and on his political relations with the senior air commanders of allied nations and CENTCOM's other components. Action taken to solve current problems served some goals and conflicted with others. Second, organizational slack shielded CENTCOM's air component from having to make latent conflict manifest. The great number of aircraft available to conduct missions reduced the likelihood that senior planners would have to trade one mission against an-

---

[40]Ibid., chaps. 2–4.

other. Lieutenant General Horner, for example, did not have to tell Lt. Gen. Walter E. Boomer (commander of CENTCOM's Marine Corps component) to divert aircraft to carry out theater-level objectives. Boomer concentrated his aircraft on supporting marines in the Kuwait theater of operations,[41] while Horner made similar accommodations for the other air forces serving in the coalition.[42]

Experience with organizational conflict indicates that organizations otherwise seriously threatened by internal inconsistencies can sustain themselves for long periods by keeping inconsistent demands apart. This separation of inconsistent policies is necessary because no organization can deal with all issues simultaneously. Pursuing intelligent and coherent strategies is difficult for organizations, and the development of strategies by subunits competing within hierarchically arranged organizations makes it difficult even to identify intelligent actions. What is optimal for each subunit or component in an organization may not be best or most favorable for the overall organization. For example, a mistaken conception of overall system optimality led Lt. Gen. Thomas W. Kelly, during the Gulf War, to resist allowing Comdr. Roy A. Balaconis to coordinate overhead imagery with Tomahawk Land Attack Missile (TLAM) strikes. Kelley may have been motivated to minimize horizontal communication to allow the most senior officers to keep better track of the activities of officers below them. Balaconis, nevertheless, proved able to provide critical and timely information to air campaign planners in theater.[43]

---

[41]W. E. Boomer, "Special Trust and Confidence among the Trail-Breakers," *Proceedings* 117 (November 1991): 50; Royal P. Moore Jr., "Marine Air: There When Needed," *Proceedings* 117 (November 1991), 63–64.

[42]Mandeles, Hone, and Terry, *Managing "Command and Control,"* chap. 3.

[43]Ibid.

Reconciling Intelligent Decisions with Organization

Common conceptions of intelligent decision making are often at odds with the actual features of organization that help achieve intelligent choice. Can we describe the relationship between organizational structure and the types of decisions generated and foster more realistic and effective organizational decision making? Such a question is pertinent to any review of Desert Shield and Desert Storm and to any consideration of future military organization because of the bureaucratic tendency to answer difficult questions with politically sanctioned slogans. Analysts will have to examine carefully the Air Force doctrine that centralized control is vital to effective employment of airpower and the many laudatory statements that have been made concerning the effectiveness of the organizational relationships set up by the Goldwater-Nichols legislation.[44]

During wartime, when the problems military organizations face are neither well defined nor well structured, uncertainty does not make intelligent choice and action impossible. How-

---

[44]The assumption embedded in Air Force doctrine regarding centralized planning and decentralized execution concerns the role of intellect in understanding all implications of the interplay among tactical, operational, and strategic tasks assigned to airpower. It is assumed that a full (i.e., synoptic) understanding of the task(s) is possible. This assumption recalls the optimism of the Age of Reason when it was believed that, if we think rationally enough and concentrate hard enough, we can solve all our social problems. That optimism is a relic of a simpler, more naive time. And, the Air Force's reference to decentralized execution is a recognition that achievement of a synoptic understanding is impossible. Interaction through decentralized execution substitutes for centralized control. Negotiation and discussion constitute processes that produce decisions in circumstances in which a decision cannot be, or is not, reached exclusively through analysis. For more on the laudatory statements concerning Goldwater-Nichols legislation see J. P. Coyne, *Airpower in the Gulf* (Arlington, VA: Aerospace Education Foundation, 1992), 153; and House Armed Services Committee, *Defense for a New Era: Lessons of the Persian Gulf War* (Washington, DC: GPO, 1992), 41–42.

ever, recognition of the pervasiveness of risk and uncertainty places a premium on robust adaptive procedures, instead of on procedures that work only when they mesh with anticipated scenarios and tasks. Ignoring risk and uncertainty may attenuate the relationship between means and ends at various decision points, either through the substitution of means for ends (goal displacement) or through premature programming. The goal displacement problem makes subjective estimates of uncertainty over time, and the way that uncertainty is handled, important concerns. Consider, for example, the conflict over what measure of effectiveness to use in estimating target damage: absolute damage (as the targeteers wanted) or functional degradation (as Lieutenant Colonel Deptula, operating in the GAT, wanted). Deptula argued, in effect, that the targeteers were engaging in goal displacement. They focused on the impact of bombing individual targets rather than on the overall efficacy of the air war in defeating Iraq.

A second implication of ignoring uncertainty—premature programming—refers to the tendency of organizational leaders to adopt a plan and order its implementation as if perfect knowledge and value consensus exist, when, in fact, they do not. Organizational members may agree on factual premises that are wrong. The resulting decisions tend to be self-reinforcing and closed to criticism. The rejection of criticism covers up existing disagreements within the organization, and the lack of consensus becomes a source of conflict—not a basis for negotiation. Despite the presence of agreement about ends, premature programming leads to self-delusion in the face of repeated error, i.e., a refusal to learn from mistakes.

Typically, organizations face many uncertainties in dealing with ill-structured tasks: key variables or parameters may be unknown (these are sometimes referred to as unknown unknowns), the magnitude or importance of known variables may be unknown, or goals and preferences may be unstable.[45] One organizational response to dealing with ill-structured decisions is to negotiate the uncertainty or problems away. In the business world, firms form cartels to set minimum prices and divide up market shares.[46] In the GAT, planners also negotiated uncertainty away by operating with a very simple model of the task environment and ignoring or eliminating complicating factors.[47]

A serious issue that GAT planners did not address in setting up their organization was the existence, location, and purpose of designed feedbacks to ensure that critical Iraqi targets were identified, attacked, and destroyed. A manager uses feedbacks to provide staff with an error signal denoting the differences between desired ends and the current situation. The GAT used very few official, formal feedback loops. The overall performance of the tactical air control center (of which the GAT was a component) was saved by the many ad hoc and informal communications links and organizations functioning as short-term error-correcting feedbacks and the skills of unit-level planners and pilots who flew their missions despite short planning periods, last-minute target and timing changes, imperfect information about the effects of previous attacks, and the normal snafus that plague combat operations. Believing the planning system would cope, Brigadier General Glosson ordered air tasking order (ATO) changes regardless of how those changes would cascade through the system and affect such operations as the

---

[45]Herbert A Simon, "The Structure of Ill-Structured Problems," *Artificial Intelligence* 4 (1973); W. R. Reitman, "Heuristic Decision Procedures, Open Constraints, and the Structure of Ill-Structured Problems," in *Human Judgements and Optimality*, eds. M. W. Shelly III and G. L. Bryan (New York: John Wiley and Sons, 1964); Allen Newell, "Heuristic Programming, Ill-Structured Problems," in *Papers in Operations Research*, vol. 2, ed. J. S. Aronofsky (New York: John Wiley and Sons, 1969).

[46]Richard R. Cyert and James G. March, *A Behavioral Theory of the Firm* (Englewood Cliffs, NJ: Prentice-Hall, 1963), 120.

[47]Mandeles, Hone, and Terry, *Managing "Command and Control,"* chaps. 2–3.

suppression of enemy air defenses or aerial refueling.[48] It is an open question whether Glosson made the system overreactive, i.e., whether his behavior induced oscillation away from understanding the effectiveness of attacks against Iraqi positions—a condition that had to be depressed by the actions of officers working at night when Glosson was away.[49]

If the Gulf War experience presages problems facing future campaign planners during combat, the single most important factor to consider when thinking about the design of military organizations is that these organizations are not immune to error. Murphy's Law operates in most critical combat situations. No matter how carefully designed and programmed, organizational components—equipment and people—will fail or violate expectations. When interdependent components, such as communications chains, are tightly coupled into serial chains, failure can cascade along them, leading to unacceptable catastrophe.[50] In the Gulf War, the U.S.-led coalition did not suffer a systemic breakdown. However, the number of daily missions and the many interdependencies among those missions caused many small breakdowns. Means to identify and mitigate errors—to degrade gracefully—should be a formal component of

---

[48]The frequency and tempo of changes ordered by GAT officers early in the air campaign may have induced a cycle of other changes over several days. Since the planning and execution of the ATO cycle involved overlapping activities, the ATO planning process was unable to reach a steady state. This matter regarding the implications of constant changes made in a process is similar to one described by W. Edwards Deming, "On Some Statistical Aids toward Economic Production," *Interfaces* 15 (August 1975); Mandeles, Hone, and Terry, *Managing "Command and Control,"* chap. 3.

[49]Informal efforts were made to prevent Glosson from overloading the TACC (Tactical Air Control Center) with changes. Maj. Mark "Buck" Rogers was designated the BCO—the Buster Control Officer. In addition, Glosson did not run the system twenty-four hours a day; his attention was limited as part of his day was spent in meetings away from the Black Hole. See Rick Atkinson, *Crusade* (New York: Houghton Mifflin, 1993), 65.

[50]F. R. Demech Jr., "Making Intelligence Better," in *C³I*, ed. Coakley, 163; Martin Landau, "On Multiorganizational Systems in Public Administration," *Journal of Public Administration Research and Theory* 1 (January 1991).

overall military design or architecture. Military organizations confronting a dangerous enemy should not have to rely so heavily on hastily formed informal communications links and ad hoc organizations to enhance the fit between means and ends.

The vast majority of information used to plan the Desert Storm air campaign was furnished by informal communications links that arose to supply battle damage assessments (BDA) and other critical and time-sensitive information to the GAT during the Gulf War. A diagram of these links would not show a clear and streamlined structure. Instead, the information ties were redundant and overlapping and linked across service lines unaccustomed to coordinating such activities in peacetime.

A very complicated ad hoc organizational architecture was built to control the large numbers of air sorties in Desert Storm. This architecture combined technology, compartmented information, numerous agencies, and people with myriad occupational specialties and perspectives and sometimes conflicting organizational responsibilities, and numerous agencies. These elements had so many linkages and pathways that even naming all the connections—let alone tracing them—may be impossible. As human-organization-machine systems become more integrated and complex, more interdependent and interlocked, the probability of tactical air control center failures increases. At some point, the system may become so complicated that Gulf War–type ad hoc organizational solutions or fixes may be inadequate.

In this context of great organizational complexity confronting Air Force doctrine relating to centralization, anticipating types of bureaucratic conflicts and preparing for their effects is especially important. As combat aircraft come equipped with more sophisticated munitions, as well as avionics, electronic warfare, communications, and sensor and targeting equipment, the associated support and logistics trails also become more complex and interdependent. The nonflying officers performing support tasks will want status, authority, and a "voice" commensurate with pilots flying missions or working in the headquarters planning offices. Indeed, they may even argue that their experience, training, and occupational specialties make them more competent than fighter pilots to exercise command of planning activities in combat increasingly driven by the necessity to integrate information quickly and accurately from a variety of sources. As will be seen in chapter 5, conflict between line and staff officers has occurred in all the services.

The story of the GAT during Desert Storm presents several compelling contrasts. First, building and executing an ATO for a static peacetime environment—in which the decision problem was clear and well structured—was very different from doing the same for a dynamic wartime environment—in which the decision problem was ill structured and less manageable. Second, there was a difference between what senior leaders and planners believed they could manage and the reality of the war. The evidence shows that formal mission-related error-correcting feedback was often inadequate or nonexistent, and communications between the GAT and the wings were often confusing.[51] The costs to the United States associated with these contrasts were low in the gulf only because we had a redundancy of aircraft and munitions, air supremacy so that attacks could be applied at will, and superbly trained and skilled pilots, air crews, and maintenance crews.

At several levels of CENTCOM's air component, key officers believed they were managing the chaos of war through planning. Yet when the activities of the many significant participants are pieced together, the reality is that neither GAT planners nor Lieutenant General Horner knew the details of what was happening in the air campaign or how well the campaign was going.[52] Planners sacrificed formal decision rationality in order to act on a timely basis. That is, they analyzed fewer

[51]Mandeles, Hone, and Terry, *Managing "Command and Control,"* chaps. 2–4.
[52]Ibid., chaps. 2–3.

alternatives and considered only the positive potential results of decisions made. Critical elements of the plan (the target sets chosen and simultaneous attack on those targets) might have been wrong (as evidenced by the fact that the Iraqi military collapse was incomplete). But these elements were not questioned.

Conclusion

In the past, when technological revolutions provided the means and impetus for significantly altered tactical and operational doctrine, few changes were incorporated into doctrine before the onset of hostilities.[53] The difficulty encountered by military organizations in developing and implementing doctrinal changes is partly a function of the extreme intellectual challenge in testing an individual weapon's effectiveness. The intellectual hurdles are even greater for evaluations of organizational architectures, where systematic comparisons and analyses of the relationship between structure and outcome are not made. There has been far more empirical research on the information-processing characteristics of individuals than on organizations and institutions.[54]

An improved analysis and communications capability depends both on the distribution of appropriate technology and the ability of personnel to use the equipment properly. The presence and distribution of particular modes of thought (e.g., the ability to respond to surprises and uncertainty), associated nonmilitary technologies, and organizational design explain

---

[53]Edward L. Katzenbach Jr., "The Horse Cavalry in the Twentieth Century: A Study in Policy Response," in *American Defense Policy*, eds. Richard G. Head & E. J. Rokke (Baltimore: Johns Hopkins University Press, 1973).

[54]James G. March, "Administrative Practice, Organization Theory, and Political Philosophy: Ruminations on the *Reflections* of John M. Gaus," *PS: Political Science and Politics* 30 (December 1997): 693.

differences among the abilities of various societies to (1) employ advanced conventional weaponry, (2) build associated logistics trails, and (3) direct combined arms warfare.[55] Organizational design reactions to new technology are often largely accidental. In the 1999 Kosovo air campaign, some air attacks became stymied because not all North Atlantic Treaty Organization (NATO) aircraft had compatible secure communications equipment. NATO pilots had to speak with each other and ground-based air controllers over open communications, thus allowing Serbian forces to monitor the conversations.[56] During the Gulf War, wide usage of secure telephones—STU-IIIs—provided the GAT with an unplanned means to direct the attacks that the units conducted centrally and on short timelines.[57] The STU-IIIs also made possible the development of many ad hoc organizations and informal communications channels, which compensated for the failures of the formal organization. Properly understood and employed in conjunction with other nonmilitary technologies, STU-IIIs offer the informal channels to exchange information and thus to conduct very rapid analysis and evaluation of the effectiveness of combined arms warfare. The expansion of communications channels and means to conduct analysis and evaluation quickly would advance the dream and past promises of great

[55]Brigadier General Glosson's view and analysis of the "Iraqi factor" is compatible with this point. The inability of the typical Arab pilot trained in the United States to respond appropriately to uncertainty or to new tasks was key to Glosson's understanding of how well Iraqi society would respond to continual air attack over a wide range of targets. Mandeles, Hone, and Terry, Managing "Command and Control," chap. 2.

[56]Dana Priest, "Serbs Listening in on Pilots," Washington Post, 1 May 1999, A1.

[57]The cellular telephone may offer a civilian analogue for the use of STU-IIIs as a means for authorities to acquire information quickly from dispersed locations. In the Washington, DC, metropolitan area, drivers (owning cellular phones) are making faster and safer commuting possible by calling police and traffic reporters with instant information about accidents and other delays. S. C. Fehr, "For Many Commuters, A Second Calling," Washington Post, 22 February 1993, A1, A6.

improvement in U.S. C², opening up an even greater gulf between the military capabilities of American forces and other
forces.

Chapter 5 will elaborate on this question of organizational
response to new technological possibilities by examining the
Navy's new operational concept of network-centric warfare.

Network-Centric Warfare

I assure you that it is utterly impossible to improvise military organizations, and it requires more than a year to build them.[1]

G en. George C. Marshall (USA) spoke the above words in December 1942, yet the sentiment applies to the recently emerging concept of network-centric warfare, which has generated a good deal of excitement in the short time since V. Adm. Arthur K. Cebrowski and John J. Gartska's 1998 article in *Proceedings* of the U.S. Naval Institute.[2] The concept of network-centric warfare entails a flatter organizational hierarchy through the widespread networking of sensors, decision makers, and "shooters." The concept promises "increased tempo of operations, increased responsiveness, lower risks, lower costs, and increased combat effectiveness"[3] and therefore must be considered as a step in the transition to a mid-twenty-first-century military. This chapter examines the network-centric warfare concept and some implications of its application in combat.

A short methodological note about evaluating new concepts must come first. A dangerous possible outcome of analysis of a new operational concept is quick abandonment if the concept

---

[1]George C. Marshall, "We Know What We Are Doing," *Selected Speeches and Statements of General of the Army George C. Marshall* (Washington, DC: Infantry Journal, 1945), 221.

[2]V. Adm. Arthur K. Cebrowski and John J. Garstka, "Network Centric Warfare: Its Origin and Future," *Proceedings* 124 (January 1998): 28–35.

[3]David S. Alberts, John J. Garstka, and Frederick P. Stein, *Network Centric Warfare* (Washington, DC: DOD C⁴ISR Cooperative Research Program, 1999), 86.

does not meet early objections or criticisms.[4] Serious concerns about interactions between network-centric organization and associated technologies lead to questions about operations. What will commanders do without appropriate information? How will commanders deal with an overwhelming number of calls for fires? How will commanders deal with technology-induced failures of the organizational architectures?[5] Others may also ask how widely the concept can be applied. For example, the entire U.S. fleet may not be able to participate fully in operations under the same network-centric assumptions. R. Adm. William J. Holland, who served most of his active military career in submarines, has noted that key elements of network-centric operations—e.g., continuous communications connectivity to transmit large amounts of data and pooling weapons assets across platforms—run counter to a submarine's defining strengths, stealth and independent operations. To counter this incongruity, the Navy will have to devise new routines and processes to incorporate the submarine into network-centric operations or accept that the submarine will no longer act independently.[6] Making the concept work over time will involve a conscious effort to invent and implement adaptations of the network-centric concept to real-world, everyday operations. It is reasonable to expect that the personnel who use the equipment will develop such adjustments to the concept. Planned experiments and operational problems that create new situational needs will likely yield new features of the network-centric

[4]For example see the criticisms of T. X. Hammes, "War Isn't a Rational Business," *Proceedings* 124 (July 1998): 22–25; Thomas P. M. Barrett, "The Seven Deadly Sins of Network-Centric Warfare," *Proceedings* 125 (January 1999): 36–39.

[5]William L. Lescher, "Network-Centric: Is it Worth the Risk?" *Proceedings* 125 (July 1999): 58–61.

[6]R. Adm. William J. Holland, "Subs Slip through the Net," *Proceedings* 124 (June 1998).

mode of operations. In the Persian Gulf War, for example, a Strategic Air Command Senior Controller, Brig. Gen. K. F. Keller, lamented that SAC strategic warning systems did not support CENTCOM. Thereupon, young SAC officers improvised a communications link to provide voice warning and data on missile launch and trajectory.[7] The 17 July to 8 August 1998 Rapid Force Projection Initiative Advanced Technology Demonstration included a large-scale experiment wherein soldiers conducted their own small experiments with the equipment. Observing these experiments, Maj. Gen. Carl Ernst, Fort Benning's commanding general, said: "when you put these technologies in the hands of these young soldiers, they will find ways to use it that we've never thought of before."[8]

While asking too much of a concept's early proponents may stymie a worthy idea, an even greater danger to understanding a new operational concept is to ask too little by failing to subject the concept to analysis of its real-world implications and consequences. Discussions of network-centric warfare frequently reference ideas, concepts, abstractions, and theories such as entropy-based modeling, chaos theory, Santa Fe Institute's complexity theory and edge of chaos, fractal mathematics, self-synchronization or self-organization, and general systems theory.[9] The ability of these ideas and metaphorical

[7]Thomas C. Hone, Mark D. Mandeles, Sanford S. Terry, *Gulf War Air Power Survey*, vol. 1, part 2, *Command and Control* (Washington, DC: GPO, 1993), 249.

[8]George I. Seffers, "U.S. Soldiers Put Personal Touch on New Technology," *Defense News* 13 (10 August 1998): 7.

[9]For examples of network-centric warfare studies that reference entropy-based modeling, chaos theory, Santa Fe Institute's complexity theory and edge of chaos, fractal mathematics, self-synchronization or self-organization, and general systems theory, see: Booz Allen and Hamilton, *Measuring the Effects of Network-Centric Warfare*, vol. 1, (company report, 28 April 1999, McLean, VA); Robert Pool, "Chaos Theory: How Big an Advance?" *Science* 245 (7 July 1989): 26–28; James Gleick, *Chaos: Making a New Science* (New York: Penguin Books, 1988); George A. Cowan, David Pines,

transfers to provide useful and practical guides to action and organization, however, is more often asserted than demonstrated.
As RAND analyst Herbert Goldhamer observed in 1958, some
of these metaphorical transfers occur more as a product of fashion or fad than a properly employed scientific tool.[10] Similarly,
casual comparisons of soccer and football or selected business
corporations, such as Wal-Mart or Deutsche Morgan Grenfell
(a financial securities firm), to the organization of combat operations assume evidence not at hand.[11] No simple statement of
similarity should be proffered (or accepted) without explicit
demonstration and searching examination of the correspon-
dence between the "things" we think we know about—e.g., soccer, football, selected business organizations, or "the edge of
chaos"—and the properties of the thing we seek to understand—e.g., warfare conducted by a network-centric combat
organization.[12]

Network-centric theoreticians' preference of explicating and
illustrating the concept through metaphors should be compared

---

and David Meltzer, *Complexity: Metaphors, Models, and Reality* (Reading, MA: Addison-Wesley Publishing, 1994); Murray Gell-Mann, *The Quark and the Jaguar*
(New York: W. H. Freeman, 1994); M. Mitchell Waldrop, *Complexity: The Science at
the Edge of Order and Chaos* (New York: Simon and Schuster, 1992); Robert Pool,
"Fractal Fracas," *Science* 249 (27 July 1990): 363–364; Stuart A. Kauffman, *The Origins of Order: Self-Organization and Selection in Evolution* (New York: Oxford University Press, 1993); Stuart A. Kauffman, *At Home in the Universe: The Search for
the Laws of Self-Organization and Complexity* (New York: Oxford University Press,
1995); Ludwig von Bertalanffy, *Problems of Life* (New York: Harper Torchbooks,
1960); and Walter Buckley, ed., *Modern Systems Research for the Behavioral Scientist*
(Chicago: Aldine Publishing, 1968).

[10]Herbert Goldhamer, "Fashion in Social Science," *World Politics* 6 (1958): 394-404.

[11]Alberts, Garstka, and Stein, *Network Centric Warfare*, 24. Alberts and his colleagues simply assert a useful analogy between combat organizations and network-
centric business organizations. They do not discuss the types of evidence required to
justify the comparisons.

[12]See Martin Landau, *Political Theory and Political Science* (New York: Macmillan,
1972), 101; May Brodbeck, "Models, Meaning, and Theories," in *Readings in the Philosophy of the Social Sciences*, ed. May Brodbeck (New York: Macmillan, 1968), 580,
583–584.

with World War II operational analysts' approach to combat problems. The methodology and results of World War II operational analysis were heavily empirical and experimental[13] and contributed positively to the operational effectiveness and capability of weapons systems in combat.[14] World War II experience showed that it is far better to apply empirical knowledge systematically to new concepts than to discover critical operational weaknesses in the heat of battle. This experience also recommends a methodological approach to understanding the concept of network-centric warfare: to probe rigorously and critically the empirical implications and consequences of the concept, and to cumulate consciously the results of these investigations.

A Precursor to Network-Centric Warfare?

No in-principle reasons suggest that the combat outcomes predicted for network-centric warfare—e.g., the collapse of an adversary's decision-making capability and attendant operational and tactical successes of one's forces—are impossible to achieve. In the 1950s and 1960s, for example, Israel Defense Forces (IDF) achieved these results without the advanced interlocking information, sensor, command and control, and engagement grids envisioned for network-centric warfare. Officers writing in the IDF journal *Maarachoth* and other sources explicitly contrasted the Egyptian mode of operations, command structure, and operational concepts with their own.[15] Maj. Gen.

[13]Jacob A. Stockfisch, "The Intellectual Foundations of Systems Analysis," P-7401 (Santa Monica, CA: RAND, December 1987).

[14]For example see Lincoln R. Thiesmeyer and John Burchard, *Combat Scientists* (Boston: Little, Brown, 1947); John E. Burchard, ed., *Rockets, Guns and Targets* (Boston: Little, Brown, 1948); and Joseph C. Boyce, *New Weapons for Air Warfare* (Boston: Little, Brown, 1947).

[15]Dan Horowitz, "Flexible Responsiveness and Military Strategy: The Case of the Israeli Army," *Policy Sciences* 1 (Summer 1970): 191-205.

Moshe Dayan, in *Diary of the Sinai Campaign*, recounted the results of this analytical process in the 1956 Sinai campaign:

> From the operational point of view, rapidity in advance is of supreme importance to us, for it will enable us to profit fully from our basic advantage over the Egyptian Army. I do not mean the advantage in quality of the individual soldier—pilot for pilot, tank crew for tank crew—but in the handling and behaviour of our entire Army and its operational formations, brigade-groups, brigades and battalions, as against those of their Egyptian counterparts. The Egyptians are what I would call schematic in their operations, and their command headquarters are in the rear, far from the front. Any change in the disposition of their units, such as forming a new defence line, switching targets of attack, moving forces not in accordance with the original plan, takes them time—time to think, time to receive reports through all the channels of command, time to secure a decision after due consideration from supreme headquarters, time for orders then to filter down from the rear to the fighting fronts.
>
> We on the other hand are used to acting with greater flexibility and less military routine. We can base our operations on units which are not interdependent, and whose commanders, receiving reports and giving the necessary orders, are right on the spot, together with the fighting men. This advantage, if we can exploit it, will enable us, after the initial breakthrough, to press on before the Egyptians can manage to adjust to the changes in their front. I am confident that we can run the campaign in such a way that the enemy will be given no time to reorganize after the assault and that there will be no pause in the fighting.[16]

IDF planners continued this line of thinking in planning for what became the June 1967 Six-Day War. In that conflict, the

---

[16]Moshe Dayan, *Diary of the Sinai Campaign* (New York: Harper and Row, 1966), 35.

IDF attacked its Egyptian, Syrian, and Jordanian adversaries' ability to think, to understand the tactical and operational situation, and to respond to Israeli initiatives. The IDF, unlike its adversaries, relied on a communications, command, and control system that provided for the autonomous operation of different combat units and different units of command. IDF commanders of small units who were directly in contact with Arab forces were able to respond quickly to emergent situations. These lieutenants and senior sergeants employed "negative feedbacks" to correct errors in their own initiatives. Their efforts focused on creating operational- and strategic-level "positive feedback" loops to impair Arab military decision making. Israeli military planning for this campaign sought explicitly to confuse Arab commanders—to increase the density of the "fog of war" they faced. This strategy increased stress on individual leaders and the fragility of the separate Arab military communications, command, and control systems.

Impressive as the 1967 victory was, Israeli analyst Dan Horowitz cautioned that the IDF strategy worked well because it exploited particular features of the Arab command structure and SOPs, military training, and social structure.[17] In contrast, the IDF approach to attacking the decision-making process and the organization of Islamic militias has proven less successful. Militia command structures and their training and SOPs are different from those of the Arab states Israel has fought through the years.[18] The Islamic militias reward initiative and compe-

---

[17]Horowitz, "Flexible Responsiveness and Military Strategy," 204–205. In a recent article, Col. Norvell De Atkine echoed Horowitz's argument but did not cite him. See Norvell De Atkine, "Why Arab Armies Lose Wars," *Middle East Quarterly* 4 (December 1999), reprinted in the *Middle East Review of International Affairs (MERIA) Journal* 4 (March 2000).

[18]The U.S. antidrug law enforcement effort parallels Israeli efforts to deal with the Islamic militias. Past success in breaking up visible South American drug-traffic organizations led to the rise of many small "atomized" drug cartels operating with sophisticated communications and encryption equipment. In effect, the drug leaders

tence in killing Israeli civilians and have applied lessons from Israel's own planning and training manuals.[19] Until recently, the Israelis sought a technological solution for combating the militias in the form of new sensor and electronic warfare technologies,[20] but militia leaders countered those measures and seem to believe that they have altered the military balance.[21] However, time is not on their side. The IDF has adjusted its strategy against the militias' command structure and the suicide-bomber tactic by developing a campaign to identify and kill militia leaders and the planners of the bomb attacks.[22]

The evolving match between Israeli operational concepts and features of the Islamic militias' command structure illustrates an important consideration for analysts as they examine new and future military organization. Operational concepts must be appropriate not only to the adversary but also to their own organization of military command.

Organization structure (e.g., hierarchy, span of control,

---

decided that a hierarchically and vertically integrated drug organization was too visible to law enforcement. The drug leaders decided to create small, specialized, flat organizations which combine—on an as-needed basis—to perform certain tasks, such as putting loads of drugs together for sale. The current antidrug law enforcement organization structure appears stymied by the drug cartel's organizational change. See Douglas Farah, "Drug Cartels Hold Tech Advantage," *Washington Post*, 15 November 1999, A1, A18.

[19]Barbara Opall-Rome, "Israel Brass Remains Committed to Deployment: Hizbollah Applies Israel, U.S. Military Strategies to Guerrilla War in Lebanon," *Defense News* 14 (21 June 1999): 4.

[20]Steve Rodan, "Israel Looks for Technology to Fight Hezbollah Guerrillas," *Defense News* 13 (14 December 1998): 18.

[21]Molly Moore and John Ward Anderson, "Suicide Bombers Change Mideast's Military Balance," *Washington Post*, 18 August 2002, A1.

[22]With each assassination of an experienced militia leader or bomb planner, the IDF reduces the intellectual capital and tacit knowledge of the militias while increasing its own relative knowledge base and experience in dealing with its foes. Unless the Palestinians change tactics or accept a ceasefire, we should expect that within a few years the IDF's assassination campaign will reduce the combat effectiveness of the militias. The militias (assuming they prefer violence to political compromise) will have to turn to more vulnerable targets outside Israel.

and division of labor) and SOPs are problem-solving devices that anticipate both the nature of problems the organization faces and the form solutions will take.[23] Not all possible organizational structures are equally compatible with their task environments nor are they equally adaptable to all types of environmental change. Indeed, over time the effectiveness of organizational structures may change, enhancing or detracting from organizational performance. Therefore, where the consequences and cost of error are high, the appropriateness of an organizational structure to its task environment should be a matter of a continual empirical review.

Studying only the causal relationship of organizational structure to combat outcomes is not enough, however. Such examinations must be linked into a coherent and more encompassing program of analysis. During the early years of World War I, the British military was poorly organized to recognize the value of machine guns and to employ them effectively.[24] Brig. Gen. C. T. Baker-Carr, who played a leading role in revising machine-gun doctrine, experienced great difficulties in the task of revising the doctrine, despite frequent German demonstrations of the gun's value on the battlefield. Baker-Carr believed that the delay in implementing changes to doctrine and force structure was the "fault of the system" (e.g., the fault of the hierarchy, the division of labor, the way analysis was conducted, and the way military problems were formulated) rather than the "fault of the individual," a conclusion with which his-

---

[23]Martin Landau, "On the Concept of a Self-Correcting Organization," *Public Administration Review* 33 (November/December 1973): 533–542; William H. Starbuck, "Organizational Growth and Development," in *Handbook of Organizations*, ed. James G. March (Chicago: Rand McNally, 1965).

[24]Earlier, the British had notable combat successes using the machine gun. In 1898, at the battle of Omduran, the British, using six Maxim machine guns, decimated Khalifa Abdullah's Dervish forces. Outnumbered 40,000 to 26,000, the British and their allies suffered 48 killed; the mahdists suffered 11,000 dead. See John Ellis, *The Social History of the Machine Gun* (New York: Pantheon Books, 1975), 85–87.

torian I. B. Holley Jr. agreed.[25] The existence of institutional and organizational processes to abet learning might have speeded widespread understanding of the machine gun's battlefield role.

Similarly, in today's context, an article published in *Proceedings* quite properly addresses a structural question about division of labor in the fleet—should information warfare be considered as a "separate and equal warfare area alongside the traditional components of the composite warfare commander structure"?[26] If this proposal is reasonable, it should be examined as part of a program of experimentation and analysis to continually assess the Navy organization's fitness for combat.

The Network-Centric Concept

Chief of Naval Operations Adm. Jay L. Johnson contrasted the network-centric concept with the existing "platform-centric" force structure, which organizes acquisition, training, and operations around "platforms"—e.g., a tank, a ship, or an airplane—or individual weapons systems.[27] In platform-centric warfare, sensor and communications networks serve to enhance the performance of individual platforms.[28] Throughout the twentieth century (and before), platforms formed the basis for building militaries, deciding what systems to buy, and determining how to employ forces and measure success on the battlefield (by counting the numbers of adversary platforms destroyed or disabled). Organizational structures employed in

---

[25]Irving B. Holley Jr., *Ideas and Weapons* (Washington, DC: GPO, 1971), 16.

[26]Erik J. Dahl, "We Don't Need an IW Commander," *Proceedings* 125 (January 1999): 48–49.

[27]Adm. Jay L. Johnson, "CNO Address at the AFCEA West," San Diego, CA, 21 January 1998.

[28]Martin Libicki and Jeremy Shapiro, "Conclusion: The Changing Role of Information in Warfare," in *The Changing Role of Information in Warfare*, eds. Zalmay M. Khalilzad and John P. White (Santa Monica, CA: RAND, 1999), 450–451.

platform-centric warfare have peaked hierarchies and separate command and communications channels for fires, air defense, strike, intelligence, and combat support. Platform-centric military organizations emphasize central planning and coordinated execution of tasks across a contiguous battlefront.[29]

The contrast between platform-centric and network-centric warfare turns on modern communications technology. In the words of Vice Admiral Cebrowski, "network-centric warfare is increasingly seen as the military expression of the information age."[30] The network-centric warfare concept was endorsed by the U.S. Joint Chiefs of Staff as a way to implement "Joint Vision 2010"[31]—the chiefs' official view of how to organize for future combat.[32] The concept has parallels in the U.S. Army's battlefield digitization, the U.S. Marine Corps' Urban Warrior experiments, and the U.S. Air Force's avionics integration and automatic data link.[33] Although each service will implement it differently, the network-centric operational concept is likely to be at the core of U.S. military planning and acquisition in the twenty-first century.

The network-centric operational concept relies on robust

---

[29]Booz Allen and Hamilton, *Measuring the Effects of Network-Centric Warfare*, 2-7 to 2-8 company report, McLean, VA.

[30]V. Adm. Arthur K. Cebrowski, "Convocation Speech," Naval War College, Newport, RI, 18 August 1998.

[31]Bill Gregory, "From Stovepipes to Grids," *Armed Forces Journal International* 136 (January 1999): 18.

[32]Joint Chiefs of Staff, "Joint Vision 2010: America's Military—Preparing for Tomorrow," *Joint Force Quarterly* (Summer 1996): 34–49.

[33]For discussion of the U.S. Army's battlefield digitization, see Barbara Starr, " 'Desert Hammer VI' Puts U.S. Digitized Army to the Test," *Jane's Defense Weekly* (9 April 1994): 17–18. For discussion of the U.S. Marine Corps Urban Warrior experiments, see Joel Garreau, "Point Men for a Revolution," *Washington Post*, 6 March 1999, A1; and Joel Garreau, "Reboot Camp: As War Looms, the Marines Test New Networks of Comrades," *Washington Post*, 24 March 1999, C1. And for discussion of the U.S. Air Force's avionics integration and automatic data link, see Gregory, "From Stovepipes to Grids," 18–19.

communications linkages among many different sensors, command nodes, and "shooters." The Navy's cooperative engagement capability system, for instance, has been designed to pass sensor data very quickly within a battle group. The fast communication enables one warship to shoot down an attacking missile by using another ship's radar data.[34] The concept combines four advanced technology domains: sensor grids, engagement grids, a high-quality information grid, and very fast C^2 processes that create a common operating picture of the battlefield and allow each unit in the network to respond to each of the threats, thereby reducing overall potential risk.

The network-centric concept, made possible by the enormous amount information generated by modern sensors and surveillance equipment and the speed with which that information may be relayed to "nodes," e.g., ships at sea, allows forces to increase the rate of decisions bearing on how to attack the adversary or respond to attacks.[35] This increase in speed of command has three effects:

1. The force achieves "information superiority" and develops a dramatically better awareness and understanding of the battle space than is obtained simply by gathering raw data. This awareness and understanding entails knowledge of the location, direction, and velocity of enemy and one's own forces. At a minimum, achieving information superiority requires excellent sensors, fast and powerful networks, display technology, and sophisticated modeling and simulation capabilities.

---

[34]Bradley Peniston, "U.S. Navy Tries Again to Install Battle Network," *Defense News* 14 (2 August 1999): 15.

[35]V. Adm. Arthur K. Cebrowski and John J. Garstka, "Network-Centric Warfare: Its Origin and Future," *Proceedings* 124 (January 1998): 28–35; see also Cebrowski, "Convocation Speech"; Robert Holzer, "U.S. Navy Must Scrutinize Network-Centric Implications," *Defense News* 13 (7 September 1998): 20.

2. A distributed force acts with speed and precision and at a great distance. Network-centric organization allows wide territorial dispersal of one's own forces so that "mass"—the concentration of combat or destructive power—is achieved by munitions on targets rather than by an aggregation of people and equipment in a smaller area. Wide distribution of forces severely complicates the coordination of an enemy's targeting efforts.

3. Improved command, control, communication, computer, and intelligence (C¹I) and connectivity offer a commander the ability to make decisions faster, to communicate decisions faster to a wider array of forces, to direct simultaneous attacks against a wider range of adversary targets, and to secure a higher responsiveness to his intent. The increase in the speed of command will shock adversary commanders with synchronized destructive events that rapidly foreclose their courses of action.[36]

Navy officials have pointed to the tactics employed in 1996 by the USS *Nimitz* and USS *Independence* carrier battle groups in the Taiwan Straits as an application of the network-centric concept. While the carriers maneuvered in traditional ways during the People's Republic of China missile tests, operations differed from the past. The admiral in charge of the operation issued only three written orders, far fewer than would have been issued before the employment of distributed computer networks. Instead of sending bulky text messages, commanders used video conferencing and exchanged detailed graphics across computer networks. The mission planning cycle was shortened from twelve hours to one hour, and different users were able to

---

[36]Cebrowski and Garstka, "Network-Centric Warfare," 32.

work simultaneously on networks to solve operational problems.[37]

Although no shots were exchanged during the missile tests, the exercise provided evidence that C⁴ISR equipment have important roles in network-centric warfare. And the role of this equipment in combat operations should increase as advancing developments in nanotechnology allow the physical size of the equipment to shrink[38]—thus reducing power and cooling requirements; increasing computational power, mobility, and portability; easing repair concerns because small lightweight replacement components can be carried by the operators; and allowing more systems to be deployed. The latter advantage, in particular, justifies a concept used to operate hundreds of nano-satellites. A payload could be divided among a cluster of small satellites, using the redundancy of many systems to ensure the performance of assigned missions.[39]

It should not be surprising that Western nations, the United States in particular, are investing in ever more complex C⁴ISR systems. At the tactical level, the intent of deploying such systems—whether as part of the network-centric warfare concept or not—is to increase the tempo of operations and the ability of military personnel to identify, target, and attack adversaries.

---

[37]Robert Holzer, "Tactics in Taiwan Cast Mold of Future Warfare," *Defense News* 12 (28 July 1997): 4.

[38]For example, David Mulholland, "DARPA Eyes Micromachines to Aid Soldiers in the Field," *Defense News* 13 (28 September 1998): 10. See also Flemming Besenbacher and Jens K. Nerskov, "How to Power a Nanomotor," *Science* 290 (24 November 2000): 1520; Robert F. Service, et al., "Atom-Scale Research Gets Real," *Science* 290 (24 November 2000), 1524–1531; H. G. Craighead, "Nanoelectromechanical Systems," *Science* 290 (24 November 2000): 1532–1535; Stephen R. Quake and Axel Scherer, "From Micro- to Nanofabrication with Soft Materials," *Science* 290 (24 November 2000): 1536–1545; Ricky K. Soong, et al., "Powering an Inorganic Nanodevice with a Biomolecular Motor," *Science* 290 (24 November 2000): 1555–1558; Leo Kouwenhoven, "Bouncing a C60 Ball," *Nature* 407 (7 September 2000): 35–36.

[39]Leonard David, "Researchers Anticipate Revolutions in Nanosatellites," *Defense News* 14 (20 September 1999): 30.

Such systems may create new combat options (or new combat vulnerabilities), including disrupting an adversary's infrastructure or his military forces C^2 (or losing operational control of one's own forces).[40] Without prejudging the effectiveness of these future technological programs, as noted earlier, the conscious adoption of a military organizational structure and an operational concept that sought to intensify the fog of war for adversaries effectively disrupted an enemy's military C^2 in June 1967.

The analytical challenges of defining the network centric operational concept may be approached at several levels of analysis. Others have identified certain challenges that must be overcome to make network-centric operations an effective operational concept. *Global 98*, a Navy wargame, for example, revealed the vulnerability of ground- or space-based networks and huge information databases to attack or disruption.[41] This vulnerability will only increase as new tools to disrupt computer systems are developed and as cyberterrorists complement these new tools with effective social engineering.[42] This chapter next examines some issues about which most analysts are silent, first exploring a few aspects of military operations from the

---

[40]Such systems are likely also to continue the well-publicized acquisition problems of schedule delays, performance shortfalls, and cost overruns. Sometimes these acquisition problems are partially acknowledged. U.S. Defense Department officials claim that they are developing the deployment schedule of a space-based missile defense system with a two-year delay from initial estimates. But new and unanticipated sources of delay will be discovered. See Dana Priest, "Cohen Says U.S. Will Build Missile Defense," *Washington Post*, 21 January 1999, A1, A10.

[41]Holzer, "U.S. Navy Must Scrutinize Network-Centric Implications," 20; Sean D. Naylor, "U.S. Army War Game Reveals Satellite Vulnerability," *Defense News* 12 (10 March 1997): 50.

[42]For an example of a new tool that can disrupt a computer system see George I. Seffers, "Stealthy New Software Enhances Hacker Arsenal," *Defense News* 14 (15 March 1999): 3, 42. As an example of a cyberterrorist's success by way of social engineering remember the "I love you" worm, dispersed in e-mails with those words in the message line, inviting readers to open the attachments, thus releasing the worm. This worm infected a very great number of computers.

perspective of human cognition and then exploring military operations from the perspective of coordinated actions in organizations.

The Person-Technology Interface

The many C⁴ISR technologies and the high operational and
personnel tempo of network-centric warfare place enormous
cognitive demands of memory, calculation, and judgment on
commanders and troops. The initial discussions of the network-
centric concept are mute about its effect on a person's ability to
perform complex cognitive operations. Yet, the network-centric
concept appears likely to increase (1) the range of topics that
commanders must consider, (2) the amount of information and
noise bearing on each topic at all levels of the organization, (3)
stress and time deadlines, and (4) the amount of time senior battlefield commanders must devote to decision making.

Under existing organizational designs, the combination of
these four factors will (1) decrease the commanders' attention
and time spent on any particular topic, (2) require additional
analytical resources to reduce ambiguity by separating information from noise, (3) increase stress and interruptions of tasks for
personnel at all levels, and (4) potentially initiate a positive feedback loop of poor decision making. Long hours devoted to the
job increase the potential for poor decision making. Research in
industrial organizations has found a marked increase in fatigue-
caused accidents as more people work longer hours over extended periods.[43] Anecdotal reports illustrate that commanders'

---

[43]David F. Dinges, "An Overview of Sleepiness and Accidents," *Journal of Sleep Research* 4, suppl. 2 (1995), 4–14; Torbjörn Åkerstedt, "Work Hours, Sleepiness and
Accidents: Introduction and Summary," *Journal of Sleep Research* 4, suppl. 2 (1995),
1–3; Torbjörn Åkerstedt, "Work Hours, Sleepiness and the Underlying Mecha-
nisms," *Journal of Sleep Research* 4, suppl. 2 (1995), 15–22.

and troops' effective cognitive performance is essential for successful combat operations and that performance is degraded by sleep deprivation. Retired Army Maj. Gen. Aubrey "Red" Newman, in several essays, recounts both personal and historical accounts of the relationship between sleep and the cognitive performance essential to command.[44] U.S. Army researchers have observed that continuous combat entails brief, fragmented sleep and that sleep deprivation impairs complex cognitive performance, including the ability to understand, adapt, and plan in rapidly changing circumstances[45]—precisely the abilities required to conduct network-centric operations and to fight "inside" an enemy's observe-orient-decide-act (OODA) loop.

Laboratory data show that people who have been deprived of sleep experience a gradual, systematic decline in cognitive performance.[46] Performance declines may have little effect on simple tasks, e.g., pointing a rifle or squeezing a trigger. How-

---

[44]Aubrey "Red" Newman, *Follow Me, vol. 1* (Novato, CA: Presidio Press, 1997), 279–288; Aubrey "Red" Newman, *Follow Me, vol. 2* (Novato, CA: Presidio Press, 1997), 193–197.

[45]Gregory Belenky, et al., "The Effects of Sleep Deprivation on Performance during Continuous Combat," *Food Components to Enhance Performance* (Washington, DC: National Academy Press, 1994); Gregory Belenky, et al., "Sustaining Performance during Continuous Operations: The U.S. Army's Sleep Management System," *Proceedings of the Army Science Conference* (1996); James A. Horne, *Why We Sleep: The Functions of Sleep in Humans and Other Animals* (Oxford: Oxford University Press, 1988); James A. Horne, "Sleep Loss and 'Divergent' Thinking Ability," *Sleep* 11 (1983): 528–536; James A. Horne, "Human Sleep, Sleep Loss, and Behavior: Implications for the Prefrontal Cortex and Psychiatric Disorder," *British Journal of Psychiatry* (1993): 413–419.

[46]Drew Dawson and Kathryn Reid, "Equating the Performance Impairment Associated with Sustained Wakefulness and Alcohol Intoxication" (pre-press manuscript, Queen Elizabeth Hospital, Australia, 1997); M. Thomas, et al., "Cerebral Glucose Utilization During Task Performance and Prolonged Sleep Loss" (paper presented at the 16th International Symposium on Cerebral Blood Flow and Metabolism, Sendai, Japan, 1993); M. Thomas, et al., "Regional Cerebral Metabolic Effects of Prolonged Sleep Deprivation," *NeuroImage* (1998): S130; D. R. Thorne, et al., "Plumbing Human Performance Limits During 72 Hours of High Task Load," in *Proceedings of the 24th DRG Seminar on the Human as a Limiting Element in Military Systems* (Toronto: Defense and Civil Institute of Environmental Medicine, 1983), 17–40.

ever, if the task is complex, unfamiliar, or accompanied by deadlines, severe failures may occur. After-action debriefings conducted by Walter Reed Army Institute of Research personnel, for example, cite sleep deprivation as a deciding factor in an Operation Desert Storm friendly fire incident. The incident involved several crews of Bradley fighting vehicles who self-reported only brief and fragmented sleep over a period of more than forty-eight hours. The ability to perform simple tasks— e.g., to lay crosshairs on a target to fire rounds accurately— remained intact, but the Bradley crew members were unable to perform more complex cognitive tasks, including understanding the tactical situation and knowing who was in front of them.[47]

The literature on the effects of stress on decision making raises additional questions about the stability and effectiveness of network-centric organization during high-tempo or long-duration operations. Stress absorbs information-processing capacity and decreases the efficiency of complex thought processes. Even small discrepancies among calculational abilities, memory, and demands for decisions create stress, and stress can produce regression to first-learned responses. Thus, more recently learned complex decision routines are more vulnerable to disruption than are older ones. Reviewing the events leading up to the ground collision of a KLM 747 and a Pan Am 747 at Tenerife, Spain, organization theorist Karl Weick observed,

> When people acquire more complex responses so that they
> can sense and manage more complex environments, [the re-

[47]See Gregory Belenky, James A. Martin, and Scott C. Marcy, "After-Action Critical Incident Stress Debriefings and Battle Reconstructions Following Combat," in *The Gulf War and Mental Health*, eds. James A. Martin, Linette R. Sparacino, and Gregory Belenky (Westport, CT: Praeger, 1996); and Stephen A. Bourque and John Burdan, "A Nervous Night on the Basrah Road," *MHQ: The Quarterly Journal of Military History* 12 (Autumn 1999): 88–97.

sponses] do not become more complex all at once. Instead they develop their complexity serially. Under pressure, those responses acquired more recently and practiced less often, should unravel sooner than those acquired earlier, which have become habitual.[48]

People at war have always suffered stress and sleep deprivation. This is neither startling nor news. However, war technologies have steadily increased the cognitive and knowledge requirements for people at all levels of combat organizations with profound implications for combat operations. Whether the technologies and the organizations that enable the technologies have exceeded some fundamental threshold for effective individual decision making and coordinated action is now an open question, which should be a fundamental concern for the proponents of network-centric operations.

It is essential to begin experiments on a person's ability to perform the types of complex cognitive tasks required in a network-centric context over a considerable period under conditions of stress and sleep deprivation. Such experimentation should reveal aspects of organizational design that may be impaired by the degradation of cognitive performance of lower-level personnel or individual commanders—and by their locations in the organization (more on this subject in chapter 6).

The Organization-Technology Interface

The deployment of advanced information-processing, communication, and sensor equipment does not present unalloyed

---

[48]Karl E. Weick, "The Vulnerable System: An Analysis of the Tenerife Air Disaster," *Journal of Management* 16 (1990): 577; see also G. Mandler, "Stress and Thought Processes," in *Handbook of Stress*, eds. L. Goldberger and S. Breznitz (New York: Free Press, 1982), 88–104.

advantages to the United States and Western states. The complexity of C⁴ISR systems creates new problems for the technology's use, its users, and the organizations in which the people and machines work. At a minimum, the deployment of such systems entails the simple but critically important assumption that combat organizations can deliver information (compatible with different equipment generations and manufacturers) to the personnel who need it at the required tempo, volume, clarity, and accuracy and without interruptions. The failure to deliver the required information can weaken combat operations and force personnel to define and solve unanticipated problems. The full organizational costs of constant access to timely information have not been analyzed adequately and are not completely understood.

The many military occupational specialties required to service and operate network-centric C⁴ISR technologies and the distribution of personnel over a very large territory require attention to organizational design issues such as information storage and retrieval, coordination, division of labor, and hierarchy. If they do nothing else, network-centric operations raise many organizational questions about the coordination necessary to conduct interagency and coalition operations. For example, the geographic location of critical network nodes imposes constraints on personnel interactions. As noted in the chapter 4 discussion of the interdiction of tankers sailing the Persian Gulf during Operation Desert Shield, communicating at great distances exposes ambiguities in the commander's intent. Given the idiosyncrasies of each encounter with the tankers, Gen. H. Norman Schwarzkopf could not decipher just what President George H. W. Bush, Gen. Colin Powell, and Lt. Gen. Brent Scowcroft wanted to do; the President and his advisors had not anticipated all possible permutations of Iraqi actions, and therefore they improvised instructions. At a minimum, the time-zone differences made it more difficult to synchronize activities between the United States and the Persian Gulf, to get the prompt and undivided attention of decision makers, and to act on their instructions.

Complex C⁴ISR systems will increase the complexity of military command organizations by creating entirely new occupational specialties. At the end of 1998 no occupational code for "computer hacking" existed within the new information operations career field.[49] Since then, however, the number of occupational specialties has increased, and it will continue to increase; this expansion of occupations will multiply the interconnections among personnel and offices—increasing the difficulty of coordinating actions and increasing specialization within existing occupational specialties.[50] Synthetic aperture radar imagery, for example, requires specially trained imagery analysts.[51] The introduction of new occupational specialties over time will increase political tensions within militaries because new roles may lead to new or different knowledge and experience requirements for command, and those people carrying out the new roles will want secure pathways to promotion and higher commands.

Advanced C⁴ISR equipment also malfunctions in ways that are difficult to diagnose—the frequency of malfunctions increases the importance of the repair and maintenance technician's skill, parts inventories, and transportation systems to move parts from the storeroom to the equipment's location. On

---

[49]Tranette Ledford, "Army Reserve Forms Cyber Defense Units," *Defense News* 13 (12 October 1998): 90. Concerns for legal constraints on information warfare deterred the United States from exercising the full capabilities of its information warriors during Operation Allied Force. See William M. Arkin, "The Cyber Bomb in Yugoslavia," *Washington Post* (online version only), 25 October 1999, http://www.washingtonpost.com.

[50]Leonard R. Sayles, "Managerial Productivity: Who is Fat and What is Lean?" *Interfaces* 15 (May–June 1985): 55.

[51]David Mulholland, "New U.S. Radar Increases Possibilities for UAVs," *Defense News* 14 (20 September 1999): 20.

occasion, equipment may suffer from multiple sources of failure, a problem that may lead to the costly removal of parts that are not malfunctioning and that may increase the amount of time that the equipment is unavailable for use.[52] High-speed operations made possible by networked C4ISR systems create new types of operational problems as well: communications transmission speed may conflict with information accuracy when use conditions or inputs change in unexpected ways;[53] speed and high-tempo operations will induce difficult-to-diagnose transient processing errors.

Operation Allied Force. The 1999 Operation Allied Force seventy-eight-day air campaign over Kosovo against Serbian forces and ethnic militias illustrates several of the issues noted above. The interaction between military organization and C4ISR technology in this campaign may invalidate some expectations about network-centric operations. As in the Navy's 1996 experience in the Taiwan Straits, video teleconferencing and secure communications played a key role in linking personnel in geographically diverse locations, e.g., military commanders of forces based in Italy, Germany, and Albania were linked with Gen. Wesley K. Clark (USA) in Belgium (strikes originated from more than twenty-two different airbases located in seven different countries[54]). Secure communications allowed the

---

[52]See Chris C. Demchak, "Coping, Copying, and Concentrating: Organizational Learning and Modernization in Militaries (Case Studies of Israel, Germany, and Britain)," *J-PART* 5 (1995): 345–376; Chris C. Demchak, "Numbers or Networks: Social Constructions of Technology and Organizational Dilemmas in IDF Modernization," *Armed Forces and Society* 23 (Winter 1996): 179–208.

[53]News organizations already have encountered a conflict between faster transmission speeds and information accuracy. The dimensions of this conflict are only beginning to be identified. While a few solutions, including better training in journalism school, have been suggested, a clear and demonstrated solution to the conflict has not yet been proposed.

[54]Frederic H. Levien, "Kosovo: An IW Report Card," *Journal of Electronic Defense* 22 (August 1999): 46.

Combined Air Operations Center in Vincenza, Italy, to be the operational center of the air campaign, while SHAPE headquarters personnel located in Belgium improvised a target-development and review process as the campaign progressed. U.S. and NATO intelligence personnel provided information about targets, and European Command's (EUCOM) Joint Analysis Center in Molesworth, England, provided targets derived from imagery taken by Hunter and Predator unmanned aerial vehicles. Military lawyers based in Germany assessed all the proposed targets in terms of the Geneva Conventions governing the laws of war, a mundane but increasingly critical example of the importance of coordination.[55] Military lawyers played a similar role during Operation Desert Shield. In that conflict, a legal advisor approved the original target list and worked with intelligence and operations personnel to ensure that the means of engaging targets met legal criteria for proportionality and for military targets. Once combat operations began, lawyers working in Riyadh with the air campaign planning staff reviewed the targets included in the daily master attack plans.[56] Military lawyers will play an increasingly important role in the choice of targets during future campaigns and will complicate the speedy transmission of targets to "shooters."[57]

In Operation Allied Force, C[4]ISR technology allowed senior flag officers to conduct long teleconferences and to choose mensurated targets in extended discussions. While this may not have occurred very often, it does demonstrate the potential for C[4]ISR to temporarily alter the hierarchy of a military organization in ways unanticipated by personnel who procured the equipment and designed the C[2] relationships. When flag offi-

[55]Michael Ignatieff, "The Virtual Commander," *New Yorker*, 2 August 1999, 33.

[56]Ted Beck, et al., *Gulf War Air Power Survey*, vol. 3, part 2, *Support* (Washington, DC: GPO, 1993), 69–70.

[57]James E. Baker, "When Lawyers Advise Presidents in Wartime: Kosovo and the Law of Armed Conflict," *Naval War College Review* 55 (Winter 2002): 11–24.

cers or senior civilians choose individual target coordinates, they temporarily ignore the larger strategic and operational concerns appropriate to their rank and they retard the ability of the tactical levels of the combat organization to accomplish their own tasks. This situation is a form of goal displacement in which flag officers transformed what they can do—examine individual target coordinates—into what they believed they should do.

The errors that are products of goal displacement in a distributed military organization arc exacerbated by the use of video teleconferences to create and discuss plans. These errors become more likely as senior leaders are further removed from the real world of making the C⁴ISR technologies work. Such errors occurred in the December 1983 raid on Libya when higher command overruled internal aircraft carrier decision making, a decision that resulted in a breakdown of internal methods for coping with error.[58] The same type of errors occurred in the teleconference-enabled deliberations leading up to the space shuttle *Challenger* launch decision. The managers who ran the teleconferences no longer had the firsthand knowledge and tacit understanding that engineers used to make the shuttle fly, and the evaluative and evidentiary criteria they placed on discussion silenced the engineers' reservations.[59] Senior NASA managers treated the engineers' silence as proof that the system was working rather than as proof that it was broken. An analogous situation could easily arise in a distributed military organization.

C⁴ISR technology also became a source of "transaction" costs for General Clark in commanding the Operation Allied Force air campaign, precisely because it allowed near-real time

[58]See George C. Wilson's description in *Super Carrier* (New York: Berkley Books, 1986), 133–154.

[59]Karl E. Weick, "Review: *The Challenger Launch Decision*," *Administrative Science Quarterly* 42 (June 1997): 395; Diane Vaughan, *The Challenger Launch Decision* (Chicago: University of Chicago Press, 1997).

communication with the political and military leaders of NATO countries that provided military forces. Clark held daily video teleconferences with NATO and then EUCOM leaders. The NATO teleconferences sometimes entailed securing civilian leaders' approval to use member states' forces or to choose particular targets.[60] The target list was a matter of intense discussion and negotiation among the political leaders of the North Atlantic Council. Phase one of the proposed three-phase air campaign contained about fifty air defense targets. The number of allowable targets increased with each of the three phases.[61] NATO air campaign planners waited until the fortieth day of the campaign to attack the Serbian electrical grid.[62] After the air campaign concluded, French President Jacques Chirac boasted that bridges remained standing in Belgrade because of his objection to knocking them down.[63] The application of sensitive U.S. assets (e.g., stealth aircraft) was discussed in separate EUCOM teleconferences because the United States was unwilling to share those assets with the rest of NATO. Targets chosen in those sessions were forwarded to the Joint Staff; especially sensitive targets were forwarded to the White House and the National Security Council staff for approval.[64]

The close collaboration of civilian and military leaders in charting the details of a military campaign made possible by advanced C⁴ISR equipment may be part of the "price" for future coalition warfare—i.e., the employment of military forces of diverse nations—and for domestic public support in each na-

---

[60]Bradley Graham, "General Says War Stretches U.S. Forces," *Washington Post*, 30 April 1999, A1; Dana Priest, "New Bomb Shorted Out Power," *Washington Post*, 4 May 1999, A1.

[61]Barton Gellman, "The Path to Crisis: How the United States and Its Allies Went to War," *Washington Post*, 18 April 1999, A1.

[62]Dana Priest, "New Bomb Shorted Out Power," A1.

[63]Dana Priest, "France Acted as Group Skeptic," *Washington Post*, 20 September 1999, A1.

[64]Michael Ignatieff, "The Virtual Commander," 33.

tion.[65] Yet, such discussions between civilian and military leaders appear to obviate the operational advantages predicted for network-centric operations, especially the commanders' ability to adapt quickly to a changing combat environment. In addition, the "price" to conduct coalition warfare may be augmented by the increased world public awareness of some facets of a campaign. The increased availability of sensors accessible by private news media organizations coupled with satellite communications reduce military leaders' ability to shape public perceptions. During Operation Allied Force, the Serbs very effectively used media organizations to shape public perceptions, which, in turn, diverted military resources and attention to answering questions framed by the media.[66]

Coordination. With respect to the internal workings of each service, network-centric operations will require the services to change the way they plan and schedule upgrades. In the Navy, for example, upgrades of entire ship classes, e.g., destroyers or aircraft carriers, are conducted in one time period. Other warships operating in the same battle group may not be scheduled to receive the same equipment until several years later. With network-centric operations, the Navy must carry out ship upgrades on all warships in a battle group, otherwise the group will not be able to operate with common data links.[67]

While the budgetary implications of procuring compatible computing, communications, and targeting equipment and software are beyond the scope of this work, some other coordina-

---

[65]Past wargames have identified maintaining political coalitions as a significant constraint on operations. Pat Cooper, "U.S. War Games Find Diplomacy May Dictate Future Engagements," *Defense News* 11 (9 December 1996): 8.

[66]Maj. Gen. Ron Keys, USAF, Briefing: Future War, n.d. (circa January 2000).

[67]Robert Holzer, "U.S. Navy Sees Initial Impact of Network-Centric Warfare," *Defense News* 13 (12 October 1998): 34.

tion issues relevant to organizational design should be mentioned.

A neglected aspect of the coordination problem is the choreography of motions in conducting attacks and defending against attacks—e.g., looking at individual computer screens, clicking on icons, or sending electronic messages. Historian E. E. Morison describes an interesting case of how choreography appropriate to a superseded technology remained after the introduction of the newer technology. In the early days of World War II, when armaments were in short supply, the British used some light artillery that had been used during the Boer War for coastal defense. However, the British commanders soon became concerned that the rate of fire of these older guns was too slow. A time and motion expert was asked to improve and simplify firing procedures. He watched one of the five-man gun crews practice and became puzzled by some aspects of the firing procedure. Viewing slow-motion pictures of the men loading, aiming, and firing, he noticed something odd: shortly before firing, two members of the gun crew stopped all activity and stood at attention for a three-second period that extended through the discharge of the gun. The time and motion expert consulted with an old artillery colonel to decipher this unnecessary pause. After viewing the film several times, the old colonel said, "Ah, I have it. They are holding the horses."[68] This example raises the questions of whether the physical or eye motions learned to operate C⁴ISR technologies in a pre-network-centric organization might reemerge with newer C⁴ISR technologies and network-centric organization when personnel are under high stress and whether this might undermine the effectiveness of operations.

Other coordination problems include creating integrating

---

[68]E. E. Morison, *Men, Machines, and Modern Times* (Cambridge: MIT Press, 1966), 17–18.

software to operate distinct systems jointly. Network-centric operations assume a great deal of communication among personnel who specialize in different warfare areas. This communication is critical to ensure that all parts of the future battle group can aid each other under shorter deadlines. Faced with the prospects of nearly continual upgrades, software integration may be difficult to accomplish. In 2000 about 150 different C⁴I systems were in the fleet. Software and protocols for linking and transferring information among all these different C⁴I systems have not yet been created.[69] The first attempts to install and run version two of the cooperative engagement capability (CEC) software on the cruisers *Vicksburg* and *Hue City*, for instance, failed due to approximately seven thousand glitches. As may be expected, some glitches were minor, e.g., some interface revisions made tracking aircraft more difficult. Other problems were major, e.g., a few systems crashed.[70] Together, the Aegis system and the CEC comprise about 5 million lines of code, and the code for each system was developed by different companies. Civilian engineers failed to anticipate the difficulties of getting the Aegis radar and weapons system to work with the CEC.

Conclusion

Combat organization and operational concepts make assumptions about features of the enemy's command structure and decision style regardless of whether the principal goal is to attack the enemy's ability to make decisions. Indeed, until C⁴ISR technologies are compatible with doctrine, operational concepts, and formal and informal military organizations, network-cen-

---

[69]Holzer, "U.S. Navy Sees Initial Impact of Network-Centric Warfare," 34.
[70]Peniston, "U.S. Navy Tries Again to Install Battle Network," 15.

tric operations cannot offer improvements over current combat effectiveness. The potential of C⁴ISR technologies and software cannot be properly examined in isolation from realistic examination of individual-technology and organization-technology interactions. Chapter 6 will compare and contrast models of organizational structures to help identify those features of organizations that may exploit the capabilities of C⁴ISR technologies.

CHAPTER 6

Comparison of Organizational Structures

The elaborate organizations that human beings have constructed . . . to carry out the work of production and government can only be understood as machinery for coping with the limits of man's abilities to comprehend and compute in the face of complexity and uncertainty.[1]

T he political decisions to reduce the number of people serving in the military have profound consequences for the operation of military C⁴ISR systems. The complexity of machines and software, the knowledge requirements to operate the machines and software, and the interdependence of tasks required to operate them and synchronize operations have reduced slack time between actions or decisions. This slack had proved to be a valuable buffer among partially autonomous units that allowed people to compensate for errors and respond to enemy initiatives, i.e., to manage the "friction of war."

The imperative to reduce size while increasing capacity for high operational tempo and effectiveness has encouraged the introduction of ever more complex C⁴ISR equipment and software into the military services. Yet, those involved in remaking the military services into "digital" organizations may not fully appreciate the human and organizational implications of their plans. The introduction of information technologies into all levels of military organizations will increase (1) the organizational

---

[1]Herbert A. Simon, "Rational Decision Making in Business Organizations," *American Economic Review* 69 (September 1979): 501.

complexity of combat organizations, (2) the interdependence between combat organizations and continental U.S.–based planning and analysis organizations,[2] and (3) the commanders' efforts to manage or control information.[3] No systematic knowledge tells us how well organizations operating complex and hazardous technologies perform nor how interdependencies, information flows, and organizational structure will be changed by incorporation of the new technologies.[4]

The national security community has yet to recognize our collective ignorance on these matters, embark on a conscious search for cause-effect knowledge, and make the necessary adjustments to take into account uncertainty and ambiguity. In 1996 congressional testimony, Gen. Charles C. Krulak (USMC) remarked that technology "will change tomorrow's battlefield in a way that none of us really understand." None of his colleagues testifying at the same Senate hearing—Adm. Jay L. Johnson (USN), Gen. Thomas S. Moorman Jr. (USAF), or Lt. Gen. Ronald V. Hite (USA)—disputed or qualified that assertion.[5] None of the senior generals testifying, however, argued for slowing the pace or altering the direction of change.

---

[2]There has always been interdependence between combat organizations and continental U.S.–based planning and analysis organizations. Yet, this interdependence will increase with the introduction of new information technologies. See for example Chris C. Demchak, "Operations without Organizations: Security Implications of Information Warfare and Military Structures" (paper presented to the Annual Meeting of the American Political Science Association, San Francisco, CA, 30 August 1996).

[3]For example, Dr. Jacob A. Stockfisch suggests that the introduction of the telegraph and the field telephone might provide interesting cases for analysis of how information technologies changed military affairs. The combination of the telegraph and railroad transportation called for the creation of the Prussian General Staff and the coordination of army groups. (Personal communication, 1 February 2000.)

[4]Karlene H. Roberts, "New Challenges in Organizational Research: High Reliability Organizations," *Industrial Crisis Quarterly* 3 (1989): 12.

[5]U.S. Senate Committee on Armed Services, Subcommittee on Acquisition and Technology, *Hearings on S.1745: Emerging Battlefield Concepts for the 21st Century and the Implications of These Concepts for Technology Investment Decisions*, 104th Cong., 2d sess., 1996, part 5.

This chapter surveys notional organizational models that may be paired with C⁴ISR technologies and describes likely errors and trade-offs that may flow from each organizational design. First it reviews the properties of individual decision making, providing greater depth to this already-discussed topic and a context for the examination of notional properties of different organizational structures. This chapter concludes with a discussion of informal organization as a means to mitigate flaws inherent in formal organizational designs.

Individual Decision Making

Network-centric operations require individuals to conduct complex and difficult tasks. Appreciating the complexity of such tasks is fundamental to proper evaluation of any organizational design for highly automated, rapid-response battle. Real-time interactions between human operators and complex computerized systems have an inherently high probability of error in any unanticipated and unrehearsed crisis situation.[6] Consequently, knowledge of how people integrate information and make decisions about complicated and rapidly changing situations is necessary to understand the impact of new C⁴ISR technologies and to minimize errors in operations. Network-centric operations and associated C⁴ISR technologies require high individual skills in (1) analyzing, evaluating, and integrating diverse information, (2) computing and calculating various options' advantages or disadvantages under stress and short deadlines, (3) negotiating courses of action with persons in other locations or commands, and (4) coordinating many actions over time to achieve tactical, operational, and strategic goals. These cognitive skills are similar to those required by persons working under

---

[6]Gene I. Rochlin, *Trapped in the Net: The Unanticipated Consequences of Computerization* (Princeton, NJ: Princeton University Press, 1997), 166–168.

current organizational operational conditions. The significant difference in the network-centric model is that a larger number of people in widely dispersed settings must have such skills.

C⁴ISR technologies, thus, have changed the meaning of "literacy" at all levels in the military, increasing the demands for sweeping knowledge and profound problem-solving skills.[7] Indeed, early in 1999, Gen. Wesley K. Clark (USA) noted that current and future operations "demand unparalleled skill and judgment on the part of all soldiers from commanders to squad members."[8] A future military network-centric organization will require "renaissance men" who have wide-ranging and deep knowledge of natural and social sciences, computers, and software (and who can "shoot"). Such knowledge is necessary but insufficient for effective operation in a military network-centric organization. Now more than ever, military personnel must have social and political skills to accomplish all sorts of tasks in organizations. Military sociologist Morris Janowitz foresaw this need in 1959 when he noted that "skill in interpersonal relations [is necessary] even more than technical competence."[9] Competing with corporations in a prosperous civilian economy to recruit skilled personnel will not be easy.[10] Nor will it be easy to retain military personnel with this highly prized competency; the range of knowledge and general managerial skills obtained in the modern (and future) military will be applicable to a wide

---

[7]For a discussion of changing literacy goals in society, see George A. Miller, "The Challenge of Universal Literacy," *Science* 241 (9 September 1988): 1293–1299; Earl Hunt, "The Role of Intelligence in Modern Society," *American Scientist* 83 (July/August 1995): 356–368; and Kirstin Downey Grimsley, "Applicants Not Making the Grade," *Washington Post*, 13 April 1999, E1, E6.

[8]Wesley K. Clark, "Meeting Future Military Challenges to NATO," *Joint Force Quarterly* (Spring 1999): 43.

[9]Morris Janowitz, "Changing Patterns of Organizational Authority: The Military Establishment," *Administrative Science Quarterly* 3 (March 1959): 492.

[10]For example see David Mulholland, "The U.S. Military Struggles to Attract Top Researchers," *Defense News* 14 (13 September 1999): 10.

range of civilian tasks and jobs. The continuation of current military service retention trends will deprive the services of personnel needed to make future network-centric-type organizations work.[11] The biggest declines in military personnel retention to date have been in the fields of communications, intelligence, and electrical and mechanical repair.[12] But regardless of whether the widespread appearance of such paragons is inevitable, critical properties of human memory, attention, and the capability to calculate options and compute courses of action may limit the effective operation of C[4]ISR systems in combat.

Over the last thirty years, behavioral scientists, cognitive psychologists, and organization theorists have established various limits to an individual's information processing, computational, and calculational abilities:[13]

[11]Senator John W. Warner recently noted that the military's most difficult problem today is keeping troops who have the skills to operate and repair high-technology weapons and computers. George C. Wilson, "Senate Chairman Pushes Unmanned Warfare," *GovExec.com*, 6 March 2000, http://www.govexec.com/dailyfed/0300/030600b3.htm. DOD civilian personnel turnover will be high and job satisfaction will be low as promotion opportunities continue to decline. Brian Friel, "DOD Reports Less Downsizing, Fewer Promotions," *GovExec.com*, 10 March 2000, http://www.govexec.com/dailyfed/0300/031000b3.htm.

[12]U.S. General Accounting Office, "Military Personnel: Systematic Analyses Needed to Monitor Retention in Key Careers and Occupations," NSIAD-00-60 (Washington, DC, March 2000).

[13]Baruch Fischhoff and Stephen Johnson, "The Possibility of Distributed Decision Making," in *Organizational Decision Making*, ed. Zur Shapira (New York: Cambridge University Press, 1997); Baruch Fischhoff, Zvi Lanir, and Stephen Johnson, "Risky Lessons: Conditions for Organizational Learning," in *Technological Innovation: Oversights and Foresights*, eds. Raghu Garud, Praveen R. Nayyar, and Zur B. Shapira (Cambridge: Cambridge University Press, 1997); Baruch Fischhoff, "For Those Condemned to Study the Past: Reflections on Historical Judgment," in *New Directions for Methodology of Behavioral Science: Fallible Judgment in Behavioral Research*, eds. R. A. Shweder and D. W. Fiske (San Francisco: Jossey-Bass, 1980); Baruch Fischhoff, Paul Slovic, and Sarah Lichtenstein, "Knowing with Certainty: The Appropriateness of Extreme Confidence," *Journal of Experimental Psychology: Human Perception and Performance* 3 (1977): 552–564; Daniel Kahneman, "Bureaucracies, Minds, and the Human Engineering of Decisions," in *Decision Making: An Interdisciplinary Inquiry*, eds. Gerardo R. Ungson and Daniel N. Braunstein (Bos-

1. People have difficulty making decisions in unique and complex situations involving risk;
2. People have difficulty diagnosing decision problems they face;
3. People perceive causality where none exists;
4. People have even more difficulty generating an adequate set of alternative actions from which they may choose;
5. People's preferences may be inconsistent, and small changes in the way a problem is posed may produce complete reversals of preferences;
6. Complex cognitive tasks involving conscious and focused thinking entail steps performed serially;
7. Little is known about decision making under the stress of emergency conditions;
8. Little is known about judgment and decision making under time stress;
9. People reduce the number of factors they consider when they have less time available for making a decision;
10. Understanding group-level decision making is not a simple matter of scaling up from individual-level decision making—group size and interactions among personnel introduce new properties to the process; and

ton: Kent Publishing, 1982); Stuart Oskamp, "Overconfidence in Case-Study Judgments," in *Judgment under Uncertainty: Heuristics and Biases,* eds. Daniel Kahneman, Paul Slovic, and Amos Tversky (Cambridge: Cambridge University Press, 1982); Paul Slovic, "Judgment and Decision Making in Emergency Situations," in *Preparing for Nuclear Power Plant Accidents,* eds. D. Golding, J. X. Kasperson, and R. E. Kasperson (Boulder, CO: Westview, 1995); Paul Slovic, "Toward Understanding and Improving Decisions," in *Human Performance and Productivity,* eds. William C. Howell and Edwin A. Fleishman (Hillside, NJ: Lawrence Erlbaum Associates, 1982); see also Kahneman, Slovic, and Tversky, *Judgment under Uncertainty;* Ronald N. Taylor and Marvin D. Dunnette, "Relative Contribution of Decision-Maker Attributes to Decision Processes," *Organizational Behavior and Human Performance* 12 (1974): 286–298; Amos Tversky and Daniel Kahneman, "Causal Schemas in Judgments under Uncertainty," in *Progress in Social Psychology,* ed. Martin Fishbein (Hillsdale, NJ: Lawrence Erlbaum Associates, 1980).

11. People may plan to use certain kinds of information in some future situations (e.g., directing forces in combat) but will actually ignore that information when it is received—that is, information seen as relevant during planning becomes less salient in the heat of battle, when there are new and unexpected cues, actions, or information.

These characteristics of human choice conflict with the implicit information-processing capabilities required to operate over several months in network-centric combat organizations equipped with C⁴ISR equipment and software.[14] People selectively perceive information. Their ability to separate information ("signals") from "noise" and to make decisions under stress, deadlines, uncertainty, and ambiguity meet only imperfectly the requirements of the effective operation of modern C⁴ISR equipment. Further, since solutions to complex cognitive tasks entail the accomplishment of tasks serially, combat leaders and personnel are susceptible to distraction from too much information and sensory overload. In the 1993 Battle of Mogadishu, those working on the command net, for example, suffered sensory overload fairly quickly, with the result that they became "strictly reactive."[15] The July 1988 shoot-down of an Iranian airliner by the USS *Vincennes* is an example in which the technological systems—the radar, fire control, and missiles—worked, but the technology-organization link failed. Stress and related cognitive failures played a role in firing the missile,[16] but

---

[14]Of course, the demands of current operations also exceed these cognitive characteristics. Yet, the new equipment will multiply the current demands on current operators.

[15]Mark Bowden, *Black Hawk Down: A Story of Modern War* (New York: Atlantic Monthly Press, 1999), 233.

[16]Baruch Fischhoff, "Testimony: On the Subject of the USS *Vincennes* Downing of Iran Air Flight 655," House Committee on Armed Services, *Iran Air Flight 655*

the primary cause of failure was the interaction of the person-technology-organizational system.[17] The organization, as a buffer between people and technologies, was inappropriately structured to help people cope with the quantity, quality, and tempo of information received, and the required analysis of those data.

Much work remains to ensure that the operation of combat organizational structures is compatible with how people process information, manage attention, respond to ambiguity and uncertainty, and make decisions. First, it is necessary to ask relevant questions. Ignoring the need to examine the compatibility of future military organizational designs with the characteristics of human decision making will only create conditions for organizational and operational failure.

Organizations and Theories of Modern Combat

Many believe that the "organization" is less relevant to effective action than the "person"; effective people will ensure the completion of required tasks regardless of the organizational setting.[18] Yet, the world is not as simple as this conventional

Compensation, 100th Cong., 2d sess., 6 October 1988; Robert Heimreich, "Testimony: On the Subject of the USS Vincennes Downing of Iran Air Flight 655," House Committee, Iran Air Flight 655 Compensation; Richard E. Nisbett, "Testimony: On the Subject of the USS Vincennes Downing of Iran Air Flight 655," House Committee, Iran Air Flight 655 Compensation; Richard W. Pew, "Testimony: On the Subject of the USS Vincennes Downing of Iran Air Flight 655," House Committee, Iran Air Flight 655 Compensation; Paul Slovic, "Testimony: On the Subject of the USS Vincennes Downing of Iran Air Flight 655," House Committee, Iran Air Flight 655 Compensation.

[17]Rochlin, Trapped in the Net, 168.

[18]See the discussion in Mark D. Mandeles, Thomas C. Hone, and Sanford S. Terry, Managing "Command and Control" in the Persian Gulf War (Westport, CT: Praeger, 1996), 155–156.

wisdom implies. Organization is an important consideration for analysis of future military operations because it provides the means for people to exercise influence and authority over others and determines the information environment and channels for individual decision making.[19] During Operation Allied Force, naval air missions proved largely successful because of improved procedures for the transmission, processing, and analysis of information. An unnamed naval official remarked: "A lot of [the success of naval strike missions] had to do with organization. . . . Some of the innovations were really how we organized ourselves better."[20] Current writing on twenty-first-century military operations, nevertheless, remains mute on the impact of organization on what military personnel do, ignoring four key issues that have been noted and described in earlier chapters.

Issue 1. Levels of Analysis. In the United States, "Joint Vision 2020," service "visions," concept papers, and some wargames conceive future battle in terms of synchronized, phased application of integrated fires guided by people using modern electronic computer, sensor, and communications equipment to coordinate closely with an information-rich headquarters.[21]

---

[19]This monograph proposes a broad view of organizational structure to include: authority relationships as reflected in hierarchical positions and responsibilities of personnel (command arrangements), communications patterns or channels, means of information storage and processing, and the factorization of decision making (or division of labor).

[20]Robert Holzer, "Report: U.S. Navy Used Arms Effectively in Kosovo," *Defense News* 14 (30 August 1999): 6.

[21]For examples of service "visions," see U.S. Navy's "Forward . . . From the Sea," (http://www.dtic.mil/jointvision/b014.pdf); U.S. Marine Corps' "Operational Maneuver from the Sea," (http://www.dtic.mil/jv2010/usmc/omfts.pdf); U.S. Army's "Army Vision 2010," (http://www.army.mil/2010/); and U.S. Air Force's "Global Engagement: A Vision for the 21st Century," (http://www.au.af.mil/au/awc/awc gate/global/nuvis.htm).

This "vision" is not new.[22] In July 1970 Gen. William C. West-moreland told a congressional committee,

> On the battlefield of the future, enemy forces will be located, tracked, and targeted almost instantaneously through the use of data links, computer-assisted intelligence evaluation, and automated fire control. . . . I am confident [that] the American people expect this country to take full advantage of its tech-nology—to welcome and applaud the developments that will replace wherever possible the man with the machine.[23]

But General Westmoreland did not speculate about the correlat-ing organizational requirements to accomplishing target identi-fication, acquisition, and fire-control tasks.

In "A Concept for Theater Warfare in 2020" and "Warfare in 2020: A Primer," policy analyst Michael G. Vickers argues that future theater warfare will take place over a larger area, at a higher tempo, by a smaller and more lethal force.[24] Electromag-netic guns, airborne lasers, and new types of munitions using millimeter wave or GPS guidance will ensure that the desired targets will be destroyed from great distances. Improvements in the scope, tempo, and efficiency of operations will result from better information guiding all-weather, day and night opera-tions using precision and long-range munitions. New mission areas will be devised and new roles and missions will be negoti-ated among the services, and these new roles and missions will provide the context for weapons systems and operational inno-

---

[22]For example see Paul Dickson, *The Electronic Battlefield* (Bloomington: Indiana University Press, 1976).

[23]Cited in Gary Chapman, "The New Generation of High-Technology Weapons," in *Computers in Battle: Will They Work?* eds. David Bellin and Gary Chapman (New York: Harcourt Brace Jovanovich, 1987), 61.

[24]Michael G. Vickers, "A Concept for Theater Warfare in 2020" (unpublished paper, OSD/Net Assessment, 24 November 1993); Vickers, "Warfare in 2020: A Primer," (Washington, DC: Center for Strategic and Budgetary Assessments, October 1996).

vation. Unmanned systems will conduct a significant proportion of tasks currently performed by people. Vickers also maintains that the introduction of new platforms may not play as profound a role in shaping mid-twenty-first-century operations as it did in mid-twentieth-century military revolutions in carrier aviation and ground maneuver. Most improvements in technical performance of military systems will result from incremental and accumulated platform advancements rather than from the introduction of entirely new systems. Technical advances will occur in stealth, mobility, and long-range precision strike.

Regardless of the imagination and coherence of Vickers's vision of future combat, he does not employ multiple levels of analysis—as discussed in chapter 3—to look at the future of war in the twenty-first century as Jean de Bloch looked at the future of war in the twentieth century. Specifically, Vickers does not examine how individual-level and organizational-level decisions are made under combat conditions, such as: (1) how people and organizations cope with "noise" and process and retrieve information; (2) how military organizations factor combat problems (e.g., the relationship between battle damage assessment and strike planning) into manageable parts and whether peacetime conceptions of combat problems properly anticipate wartime conditions; (3) how combat organizations ensure quality of analysis; or (4) how people and organizations coordinate actions under tight deadlines and high individual stress. Vickers is not alone in omitting these levels of analysis.[25] What little official writing exists on information storage and processing, division of labor, command arrangements, span of control, coordination of information and analysis, and personnel skills offers inadequate guidance for the twenty-first century. As

---

[25]A notable exception to the neglect of levels of analysis in military analysis is the work of Lt. Gen. Philip D. Shutler (USMC, ret.). See Philip D. Shutler, "Thinking about Warfare," *Marine Corps Gazette*, November 1987, 18–26.

noted previously, it is assumed that the forward and backward distribution of information, instructions, feedback, and evaluations—i.e., close coordination of tactical and command units or greater interdependence between the theater and organizations located in the continental United States—will be seamless. This assumption is equivalent to postulating a functioning frictionless organization—an organization without error—conducting flawless operations under the most dangerous, stressful, rapidly changing, and uncertain conditions.

During combat many opportunities for confusion or communications breakdowns at all organizational levels, especially among tactical units, arise, even when the equipment is functional. During the 1993 Battle of Mogadishu, for example, a Ranger captain refused two separate opportunities (due to personal pique) to speak via radio with a delta team leader to coordinate their response to Somali attacks,[26] and the flow of information between commanders flying overhead and the convoys did not enhance situational awareness of either group. As reporter Mark Bowden wrote:

> High above the fight, commanders watching out their windows or screens couldn't hear the gunfire and screaming of wounded men, or feel the impact of the explosions. From above, the convoy's progress seemed orderly. The visual image didn't always convey how desperate the situation really was.[27]

Information flow between the theater and organizations located in the United States was not seamless in either the 1990–1991 Persian Gulf War or the 1999 Operation Allied Force. In both operations, many "disconnects" occurred between organizations in the United States and in the theater. The very com-

[26]Bowden, *Black Hawk Down*, 239.
[27]Ibid., 113.

plexity of modern military organizations almost ensures high coordination costs and communications breakdowns in large-scale operations.[28] The same conditions have pertained to smaller or shorter operations as well, e.g., the efforts to seize Somali warlords or to free the crew of the USS *Mayaguez*.[29]

Issue 2. Exercise of Authority. Explicit examination of future military organizational design raises questions about how authority will be exercised when tasks and responsibilities are defined by ever-increasing knowledge requirements. "Joint Vision 2020" and the service visions do not address whether and how C⁴ISR equipment will affect rank-based military authority.

The ability to engage many widely dispersed civilian and military leaders quickly has reached new levels, and future improved communications technology will impose high-level scrutiny at ever-lower organizational levels, increasing the reach of civilian authorities into operational decisions. Consequently, the need to coordinate civilian approval or the veto of plans or targets will slow planning decisions. In the immediate aftermath of NATO's air campaign against Serbia, for example, Russian troops occupied the Pristina airfield in Kosovo. General Clark sought to prevent the first two hundred Russians from flying in reinforcements, ordering Lt. Gen. Michael Jackson, a British officer, to block their arrival. Jackson refused the order, and appealed to senior British military and civilian officials in London, who persuaded Clinton administration officials to drop General Clark's plan. Gen. Henry H. Shelton (USA), the Chairman of the Joint Chiefs of Staff, received a 4:00 A.M. tele-

---

[28]Mark D. Mandeles, Thomas C. Hone, and Sanford S. Terry, *Managing "Command and Control"* in the Persian Gulf War (Westport, CT: Praeger, 1996). The 7 May 1999 accidental bombing of the Chinese Embassy in Belgrade is described by Michael Ignatieff, "The Virtual Commander," *The New Yorker*, (2 August 1999), 34.

[29]Bowden, *Black Hawk Down*; John F. Guilmartin Jr., *A Very Short War: The* Mayaguez *and the Battle of Koh Tang* (College Station: Texas A&M University Press, 1995).

phone call from his British counterpart, Gen. Sir Charles Gu-
thrie, to request his support in overturning General Clark's
plan.[30]

New command, control, and communications technologies
will make such challenges more common and make it necessary
to pay attention both to the effect of senior leaders on their subordinates and to the effect of personnel at lower organizational
levels on senior and mid-level personnel. Civilian political leaders have challenged military authority many times, and these
situations are the raw material of leadership studies and evaluations. These technologies also will lead to a historic reversal of
authority relationships in some parts of the military or with respect to some tasks. In 1959 Morris Janowitz argued that as U.S.
military organizations have grown more complex, their authority systems have become "less arbitrary, less direct, and even
less authoritarian."[31] Janowitz's observation, however, may no
longer hold. In Operation Allied Force, senior leaders altered
the existing authority relationships with their staffs by devoting
hours-long video teleconferences to choosing individual precision-guided munition's desired mean points of impact. In doing
so, senior leaders made a mockery of the concept of task delega-
tion and undermined the initiative of their targeteers. The impact of C[4]ISR technologies on leader-subordinate authority
relationships also affects middle levels of management; lower-
level personnel may use e-mail to bypass mid-level chains of
command in seeking or providing information to senior levels.[32]
The new C[4]ISR technologies permit a more varied set of leader-
subordinate relations.

---

[30]Bradley Graham, "NATO Insubordination in Kosovo is Recalled: General's Orders Disregarded, Shelton Says," *Washington Post*, 10 September 1999, A33.

[31]Janowitz, "Changing Patterns of Organizational Authority."

[32]In *Black Hawk Down*, Bowden describes several examples of noncommissioned officers making decisions and taking actions that bypassed or circumvented the authority of commissioned officers.

Issue 3. Impact of Numbers and Types of Occupational Specialties. As we saw in chapter 5, "Joint Vision 2020" is silent about the impact of greater functional specialization of military occupations on tactical combat operations and organizations as ever more complex equipment becomes integrated into the force structure. The functional specialization and structural differentiation—i.e., the larger number of military occupational specialties—required to operate, maintain, and service complex C^4ISR equipment and software includes not only the operation and maintenance of new equipment and software but also the integration of different types of equipment and software.[33]

In the past, as new skills were required to operate new weapons, new forms of military organization and professional societies arose.[34] In the late 1940s, for example, Hsue-shen Tsien (now known as Qian Xuesen) proposed the establishment of a "Jet Weapons Branch" to control ballistic missiles in combat and a society for the advancement of jet propulsion. In his memoir, famed aerodynamicist Theodore von Kármán noted that Tsien's proposal was quite right; the skills required to conduct missile operations were different from those required to operate existing weapons.[35]

It is often assumed that advanced C^4ISR technologies will reduce the requirement for numbers of personnel, but this assumption may soon be disproved. The "face-to-glass" ratio[36]—

---

[33]For example, Gen. Robert T. Herres proposed a new occupational specialty to cope with the complexity of C^2. See Thomas P. Coakley *Command and Control for War and Peace*, with an introduction by Herres (Washington, DC: NDU Press, 1992), xvii.

[34]The post–World War II military personnel specializations in electronic warfare are associated with the Association of Old Crows.

[35]Theodore von Kármán with Lee Edson, *The Wind and Beyond* (Boston: Little, Brown, 1967), 309.

[36]The "face-to-glass" phrase was coined by Cdr. Dan Proctor, Intelligence Officer, USS *George Washington*, in a briefing, "Carrier Intel Support for Precision Strike," 31 October 1999, unclassified.

that is, the number of people required to look at monitors and screens—may increase. The new occupational specialties will complicate the interactions among people and increase the difficulty of coordination of organizational components. The proliferation of occupational specialties made necessary by complex person-machine-organization interactions make system stability a greater concern for senior leaders. The increasing complexity of person-machine-organization systems will be accompanied by greater interdependence among the components of those systems, which lead to unscheduled system crashes and surprises. Surprises, by definition, make the behavior of the whole system less predictable, and thus reduce command situational awareness and lower senior leaders' ability to control their forces in combat. To the extent that peacetime reorganizations seek to create a streamlined and efficient organizational structure to save money or to reduce personnel, the elimination of duplicative units (e.g., the retirement of the EF-111A Raven) increases the overall vulnerability of complex person-machine organizations to the unanticipated and unexpected. The sources, numbers, and types of errors that will be seen in combat are rarely recognized during peacetime. In combat, when those errors appear in one locality, they have repercussions in other parts of the organization as adjustments become required. In this manner, errors may flow through the organization, increasing the vulnerability of forces and plans to adversary initiatives.

Issue 4. Management Trade-offs. Waging warfare with modern communications, sensors, and computing equipment, complex weapons systems, and long-range precision munitions requires organizational forms that (1) conserve the attention of senior leaders, (2) do not overwhelm the average user's computational and calculational abilities, and (3) respond well to uncertainty and rapid changes. Official documents such as "Joint Vision 2020" fail to acknowledge that the increasing complexity of person-machine-organization systems both solve and create combat leadership problems. The new means of waging combat thus confront military leaders with major management trade-offs and decision paradoxes in the design and operation of their organizations. Failure to anticipate how machines and people will work within their twenty-first-century organizations will endanger the achievement of military missions and national policy, just as surely as failure to acknowledge the reality of the fire-swept zone resulted in many World War I deaths.

To begin to develop a picture of an effective twenty-first-century military organization, the following sections explore the impact of notional organizational structures on how people and machines work. These notional organizations are "ideal types"; they don't describe actual organizations. Together they make up a comparative typology against which real organizations may be described and measured.

Tightly Coupled Organization

Tight and loose coupling are end points on a scale describing an important feature of organizational structure: the interrelationship among organizational components and processes.[37] Tight coupling obviates the use of multiple and alternative channels and requires that processes work in a fixed order. In contrast, loose coupling allows a set of components or relationships among procedures to be changed; alternatives are available.[38] These end points do not describe actual organizations; real or-

---

[37]Dan Horowitz's description of Israeli combat organization and operations in the June 1967 war also illustrates well the distinction between tightly and loosely coupled organization. "Flexible Responsiveness and Military Strategy: The Case of the Israeli Army," *Policy Sciences* 1 (Summer 1970): 191–205. See also the analysis of how Israeli forces overcame many weaknesses in the October 1973 war in Anthony H. Cordesman, *The Arab-Israeli Military Balance and the Art of Operations* (Lanham, MD: University Press of America, 1987), 43.

[38]Eliot A. Cohen and John Gooch, *Military Misfortunes: The Anatomy of Failure in War* (New York: Vintage Books, 1991), 23.

ganizations will be found at varying positions along the scale.[39]
Organizational subunits may also differ in the degree to which
they link processes and relationships. During the Persian Gulf
War, portions of Central Command's air component (CEN-
TAF) operated at different positions on the tightly/loosely
coupled scale on different days.

For example, the GAT cell developed a very detailed plan
for the first few days of the air campaign that was intolerant of
deviation. As the war proceeded, however, the GAT allocated
unspecified sorties to attack strategic and mobile "targets of opportunity." The relationship between the GAT and intelligence
agencies also illustrates how tightly coupled and loosely coupled processes may coexist. The connection between the GAT
and the CENTAF intelligence agency was formal; the passage
of information between the two was constrained and involved
the use of prescribed procedures, processes, and personnel. Simultaneously, the relationship between the GAT and intelligence agencies based in the United States was much looser, with
many informal contacts at various hierarchical levels and few
prescribed constraints on the communication of information.
Lt. Gen. Charles A. Horner unintentionally referred to the coupling concept when he contrasted planning for conventional
war—in which one manages chaos and assumes the necessity of
deviating occasionally from daily ATOs—and planning for nuclear war—in which the commander uses a detailed script to assign aircraft to targets and assumes deviations from the ATO
represent errors.[40]

In tightly coupled organizations, rank—one's position in
the organizational hierarchy—and the formal authority that
flows from rank allows superiors to determine the decision

---

[39]See Carl G. Hempel, "Typological Methods in the Social Sciences," in *Philosophy
of the Social Sciences: A Reader*, ed. Maurice A. Natanson (New York: Random
House, 1963), 213.

[40]Mandeles, Hone, and Terry, *Managing "Command and Control,"* chap. 3.

premises and actions of subordinates.[41] In such organizations, planning and execution are linked in a linear sequence: goals are enunciated at higher levels, translated into specific plans and policies by mid-level personnel, and executed by designated personnel. In this process, portions of the plans are reduced to standard administrative procedures, such as special instructions (SPINS) or rules of engagement (ROE). Once issued, commands are executed by diligent subordinates following prescribed processes, schedules, and timetables. The organization's structure, which includes numbers of levels, span of control (the numbers of people supervised) at each hierarchical level, specialization of roles, and division of labor, may be viewed as a "theory." This organizational theory anticipates and predicts problems the organization may face. As noted organization theorist Martin Landau notes, the organizational structure itself provides the solution to those organizational problems in the form of decision rules, routines, or SOPs.[42] In a tightly coupled organization, the arrangement of decision rules, routines, or SOPs to coordinate and integrate actions represents knowledge about the environment and problems the organization confronts.[43]

Employing tightly coupled organizations in certain environments or tasks has its clear advantages. Such organizations (1) deal with well-structured problems or can convert ill-structured problems into well-structured ones; (2) assign problems to subunits in a well-defined way, with an explicit division of

---

[41]Leonard D. Sayles, "Technological Innovation and the Planning Process," *Organizational Dynamics* 2 (Summer 1973): 68–80.

[42]Martin Landau, "On the Concept of a Self-Correcting Organization," *Public Administration Review* 33 (1973): 533–542; William A. Starbuck, "Organizational Growth and Development," in *Handbook of Organizations*, ed. James G. March (Chicago: Rand McNally, 1965).

[43]Martin Landau and Eva Eagle, "On the Concept of Decentralization" (unpublished paper, Institute for Governmental Studies. Berkeley: University of California, 1981).

attention and labor among subunits; (3) use clear sets of procedures to deal with conflict between subunits; and (4) encompass
clear information requirements associated with choices. When
dealing with well-structured problems, the relationship between
means and ends is unambiguous and understood, and performance can be evaluated. The decisions may be "programmed" in
the sense that a program or set of rules, as in a computer program, governs a correct decision.[44] For March and Simon, "the
term program is not intended to connote complete rigidity. The
content of the program may be adaptive to a large number of
characteristics of the stimulus that initiates it."[45]

Programmed decisions appropriate to tightly coupled organizations require agreement on both preferred outcomes (or
ends or values) and appropriate means (or methods or tools).
When agreement regarding a task or problem is obtained, the
solution may be delivered as a detailed prescription that governs
the sequence of system responses to a complex task environment. Developing alternatives, bargaining, or negotiating is unnecessary. There is no doubt about goals or ends, and the
knowledge and technology needed to achieve the ends are available. The promise of programmed decision making as a means
to solve problems is so powerful that it is presented as a norma-
tive ideal—as the most legitimate mode of decision—even when
programmed decision making is not possible.[46] Unfortunately,
the range of tasks for which programmed decisions are appro-

[44]James D. Thompson and Arthur A. Tuden, "Strategies, Structures, and Processes
of Organizational Decision," in *Comparative Studies in Administration*, eds. J. D.
Thompson and A. Tuden (Pittsburgh: University of Pittsburgh Press, 1959); Martin
Landau, "Decision Theory and Comparative Public Administration," *Comparative
Political Studies* 1 (July 1968): 175–195.

[45]James G. March and Herbert A. Simon, *Organizations* (New York: John Wiley and
Sons, 1958), 142.

[46]David Braybrooke and Charles E. Lindblom, *A Strategy of Decision* (New York:
Free Press, 1963).

priate is very small.[47] As Nobel laureate Herbert A. Simon notes, "Many, perhaps most, of the problems that have to be handled at the middle and high levels in management have not been made amenable to mathematical treatment, and probably never will."[48]

Civilian and military leaders often prefer tight coupling, peaked hierarchy, and programmed decision making because these organizational features promise that their ideas and intentions will be implemented faithfully and reduce the costs of communication with subordinates. Theoretically, under conditions of certainty about the environment and the effectiveness of organizational responses, hierarchy speeds implementation of orders by reducing (1) the time required to transfer instructions and (2) negotiation costs—the need to negotiate, discuss, or clarify orders. Table 6-1 summarizes the properties of tightly coupled organizations.

Features of Future Operations. As argued above, an organization may employ several different decision strategies simultaneously. A loosely coupled structure may be used to deal with rapidly changing circumstances, and a tightly coupled structure

---

[47]The issue also has been dealt with at great length in the complementary research of philosopher of science Karl R. Popper and Nobel laureate economist Friedrich A. von Hayek. Both saw their research during and before World War II as efforts to analyze and undercut the desirability of planning philosophies to guide society. For von Hayek, the prime argument in favor of markets was not grounded in ideology; it was based on recognition of the cognitive limits of central planners. For Popper, the prime philosophical argument against planning centered on epistemology: on the limits of what even a perfect planner could know. Friedrich A. von Hayek, *The Road to Serfdom* (Chicago: University of Chicago Press, 1944); Hayek, "The Use of Knowledge in Society," *American Economic Review* 35 (September 1945): 519–530; Karl R. Popper, *The Poverty of Historicism* (New York: Harper Torchbooks, 1957); Popper, *The Open Society and Its Enemies: The Spell of Plato* (Princeton, NJ: Princeton University Press, 1971); Popper, *The Open Society and Its Enemies: The High Tide of Prophecy* (Princeton, NJ: Princeton University Press, 1971).

[48]Herbert A. Simon, *The Shape of Automation for Men and Management* (New York: Harper and Row, 1965), 58–59.

TABLE 6-1.
Notional Structural Properties: Tightly Coupled Organization

Features	Properties
Coordination	• an organization chart provides a picture of a clearly defined sequence of actions in a single fixed order (no alternative channels) • planning and execution are linked in a linear sequence
Error Correction Strategies	• redundancy is low • preconceived plans and programs are assumed to be adequate to task(s)
Hierarchy	• the division of labor is well defined • the span of control narrows rapidly toward the top of the organization
Potential Errors Generated by Structure	• premature programming (no guarantee that program is adequate to task[s]) • uncertainty absorption • uncertainty negotiated away • lower attention to the relationship of means to goals may breed goal displacement
Structure-Problem Match	• superiors determine the actions of subordinates • the division of labor and specialization anticipates and predicts problems faced • the model is appropriate for well-defined and well-understood tasks • the model is inappropriate for poorly understood or unclear problems
Implications of Tightly Coupled Organization for Coordination of Long-Range Precision Fires	• decoupling of specified Long-Range Precision Fires Command from theater combat operations cause-effect knowledge relating fires to military and political outcomes is assumed • senior civilians have more control of goals of strategic operation and oversight of operations • new coordination costs between theater combat organization and a specified Long-Range Precision Strike Command

C⁴ISR Technology Effects

- senior-level civilians have more oversight of operations
- personnel at all levels, including senior military leaders, operate at higher tempo as they take on more tasks
- organizational complexity increases as the number of occupational specialties increases; the need for increased numbers of personnel grows
- the difficulty of coordination increases
- organizational fragility increases as complexity and coordination costs rise; senior leaders have less assurance of their situational awareness of own forces
- informal organizations are more important to operation's success

may be used to solve well-defined and clear tasks for which appropriate and effective knowledge and technologies have been developed. The arrangement of decision rules, routines, or SOPs in tightly coupled organizations (or organizational subunits) to coordinate and integrate actions presupposes knowledge that matches means with ends. In this context, effective long-range precision strike operations against strategic targets assume two peacetime organizational actions:

1. Creating a specified Long-Range Precision Strike Command separate from the joint force commander—a dedicated, tightly coupled organization (that may be deployed to the unified combatant commands) to mesh strike operations with a variety of sensors and information-analysis infrastructure—well in advance of a conflict
2. Creating a dedicated interdisciplinary research and analysis component of the specified command, to supply the cause-effect knowledge necessary to operate a tightly coupled organization

The operational advantages to decoupling strategic long-range precision strike from the continuing operations of a joint or unified force commander relate to focusing the commander's attention on critical tasks and to the knowledge requirements to conduct precision strikes effectively, and include the following:

1. Decoupling strategic operations from a unified commander reduces theater logistics requirements and permits the joint commander to focus more attention on the enemy's military forces that are in contact with U.S. forces

2. The steep knowledge requirements for identifying, tracking, and acquiring certain strategic target sets may be developed during a conflict or during a short "build-up" to a conflict;[49] too many competing interests and perspectives prevent the necessary information gathering and experimentation.[50] Decoupling strategic operations from a unified commander concentrates the knowledge-producing resources for attack and reduces the transaction costs in the transmission of relevant information.

---

[49]Despite heroic efforts, the knowledge required to attack Iraqi mobile missiles during Desert Storm was not developed. The Iraqi facilities that built Scuds were vulnerable to conventional air attack because they were difficult to hide. However, the mobile launchers and decoys, the missile assembly areas that supported them, and the logistics that sustained them were very difficult to locate or track. Yet, it was precisely those activities and areas that air forces were asked to attack.

[50]For example, during Desert Storm, Marine Capt. Scott Ritter traveled to Ar Ar, a commando staging base in western Saudi Arabia, to propose a plan for a covert team to infiltrate southwestern Iraq. Ritter would accompany commandos on missions to collect the debris of a bombed decoy in hopes of developing a radar "signature" that could be used by Air Force bombardiers to distinguish fake Scuds from real ones. One night, while Ritter was planning a reconnaissance mission, an officer from Central Command (CENTCOM) headquarters arrived with a direct order from Gen. H. Norman Schwarzkopf to abort the work and depart. The officer called Ritter "a defeatist, trying to ruin the morale of the operators." Schwarzkopf apparently believed that operator morale was more important than learning how to defeat the mobile missiles. Barton Gellman, "A Futile Game of Hide and Seek: Ritter, UNSCOM Foiled by Saddam's Concealment Strategy," *Washington Post*, 11 October 1998, A01, A39–40.

3. A dedicated interdisciplinary research and analysis agency will be an essential component of a specified Long-Range Precision Strike Command; its tasks and purpose will be different from that of developing doctrine and tactics.[51] The prime responsibility of this research component is to identify categories of targets (or target sets) and conduct causal analyses of their relationship to military and political goals. The research component will include natural and social scientists and historians and look much more like a World War II operational analysis group than a contemporary systems analysis group.[52]

Creating a separate analysis branch to support long-range precision strike will not be easy while avoiding the implications of Gresham's Law of Planning—i.e., planned action drives out unplanned actions, thus reducing organizational fitness to solve unanticipated problems.[53] Other practical design problems in creating such an analysis shop will require constant oversight,

---

[51]The mission of the Navy's new Network Centric Innovation Center will address tactics and doctrine—essential components of figuring out how to operate in new ways. However, tactics and doctrine do not address the broader problem of understanding how to connect U.S. military actions with goals. For a discussion of the Navy's new Network Centric Innovation Center, see Robert Holzer, "U.S. Navy Will Establish 'Network Centric' Center," *Defense News* 14 (15 November 1999): 28.

[52]According to former Director of Central Intelligence George C. Tenet, the dispersion of analytical talent to tasks other than the construction and maintenance of databases has routinely been "accorded a low priority and often overlooked in production planning and scheduling." He added that database production is one of the first activities curtailed when resources are limited and leadership attention to such issues is "infrequent, episodic, and essentially reactive." See Tenet, "DCI Statement on the Belgrade Chinese Embassy Bombing," House Permanent Select Committee on Intelligence, Open Hearing, 22 July 1999, http://www.cia.gov/cia/public_affairs/dci_speech_072299.html, accessed 1999.

[53]This argument does not imply that deliberate planning is a waste of time. A commitment to planning has different consequences for the efficiency of daily operations in a known environment than it has for the ability of an organization to handle unanticipated situations.

and some of these problems may be unresolvable over the long term. For example, the analysis shop will have difficulty proposing experiments if failure means cancellation of new acquisition programs. The analysis shop's relationship to the larger operational command will always be sensitive. No one should expect an operational command to fund long-term basic research, but such research is a necessity. If the shop's analysts are effective, other military components will place demands on their time for advice and help. The long-range precision strike analysis shop will have to avoid becoming entangled in activities that have very short deadlines. If the analysis group is isolated from the daily affairs of the specified long-range precision strike command, however, it becomes difficult for its analysis to influence operations.

Creating the knowledge required to incapacitate a potential adversary's military and governmental system is a labor-intensive process; it entails conducting longitudinal and theoretically driven applied research that integrates widely disparate perspectives on how societies and their militaries function and operate and new methodologies to test the resulting hypotheses.[54] A Long-Range Precision Strike analysis organization must be part of a network having strong formal and informal links with the military services, intelligence agencies, wargaming and simulation agencies, and war colleges so that information may be shared and concepts tested. Interaction among many institutions engaging in related analytical work is essential; learning

---

[54]The question remains open whether the air campaign theoreticians correctly identified the target sets that enabled Saddam Hussein to engage in war. In the "Instant Thunder" briefing, Col. John A. Warden III estimated that only six days of air combat would be necessary to incapacitate the Iraqi military. Yet, six days of bombing was not enough to force Saddam Hussein to surrender. The conditions under which a bombing campaign, using conventional high-explosive munitions, may force a regime to surrender simply are not known. But this type of cause-effect knowledge is indispensable for a militarily successful strategic campaign.

how to do new things requires the capability to interact.[55] The boundaries between the different agencies linked in a network would be permeable and fluctuate—in response to a changing environment—a situation enhanced by (1) a personnel exchange program, (2) the rapid rotation of officers as they are promoted, and (3) a future variant of the Joint Force Command's "Knowledge Today" intranet.[56] Hence, there should be constant and ongoing efforts to manage the process in action, to respond to informal processes of subgroup formation and linkages that develop.[57] A network of agencies solves the kinds of interorganizational problems—e.g., how to create and diffuse new knowledge—that cannot be met easily and effectively by a single organization.[58]

Some of the required knowledge for long-range precision strikes may come from very highly classified sources. It would be most efficient to dedicate full-time career personnel with appropriate clearances to the work of identifying the causal connections between target sets and military actions so that they will have ready access to the necessary classified information.

The knowledge requirements for the application of tightly coupled organization structure to combat are unyielding. Despite the advantages of reducing anxiety by presenting an ap-

---

[55]Mark D. Mandeles, *The Development of the B-52 and Jet Propulsion* (Maxwell AFB, AL: Air University Press, 1998); Thomas C. Hone, Norman Friedman, and Mark D. Mandeles, *American and British Aircraft Carrier Development, 1919–1941* (Annapolis, MD: Naval Institute Press, 1999); Louis Galambos with Jane E. Sewell, *Networks of Innovation: Vaccine Development at Merck, Sharp and Dohme, and Mulford, 1895–1995* (New York: Cambridge University Press, 1995).

[56]George I. Seffers, "New U.S. Command Adopts Unorthodox Structure," *Defense News* 14 (1 November 1999): 25.

[57]Paul 't Hart, "From Analysis to Reform of Policy-making Groups," in *Beyond Groupthink: Political Group Dynamics and Foreign Policy-Making*, eds. Paul 't Hart, Eric K. Stern, and Bengt Sundelius (Ann Arbor: University of Michigan Press, 1997).

[58]See Robert Agranoff and Michael McGuire, "Multinetwork Management: Collaboration and the Hollow State in Local Economic Policy," *J-PART* 8 (January 1999): 70, 85.

pearance of certainty to outsiders and within one's own organization, employment of tightly coupled decision systems is problematic in uncertain or rapidly changing circumstances. Under the more normal and ubiquitous conditions of ambiguous and imperfect information, risk, and uncertainty in combat, leaders who prefer to use a tightly coupled, programmed decision strategy for all missions forego the opportunity to learn about the differences between the objective properties of their combat environment and the organizational model of that situation. The act of programming a solution to a task is not a guarantee that the program itself is adequate to the task, a factor not usually acknowledged by partisans of a plan. Such behavior merely promotes self-delusion.

Several generic types of organizational errors may impair future military operations of the sort described by Michael Vickers above when conducted by tightly coupled organizations. First, the synchronization and scheduling of actions and the coordination of many different personnel and offices create a vulnerability to random accidents and intended adversary actions. In *Normal Accidents*, sociologist Charles A. Perrow argues that disturbances can propagate quickly and cascade throughout a tightly coupled system, causing severe dislocations and problems.[59] Tightly coupled organizations offer fewer opportunities to recover once a severe error appears and begins to create failures elsewhere in the system. The *Challenger* space shuttle explosion resulted from a set of interrelated and connected errors of the kind that may easily occur in combat. The standard means to find potential errors before they become manifest have limited effectiveness in tightly coupled organizations. Even when technical experts have time to identify and examine potential error signals in a "well-attended meeting prior to putting the technology into action, their interpretation of the

---

[59]Charles A. Perrow, *Normal Accidents* (New York: Basic Books, 1984).

signals is subject to errors shaped by a still-wider system that includes history, competition, scarcity, bureaucratic procedures, power, rules, and norms, hierarchy, culture, and patterns of information."[60]

The 7 May 1999 bombing of the Chinese Embassy during Operation Allied Force was an error born of poor targeting procedures, inadequate review, and faulty databases—all of which were made more likely by information flow in a tightly coupled organizational structure.[61] Neither the CIA analyst who doubted whether the embassy building was the desired arms agency target nor the officer on the European Command's targeting task force raised their concerns with higher-level officials, and these high officials were ignorant of their own ignorance.[62] Consequently, those making the final decisions did not have the appropriate knowledge to support their decisions.

Loosely Coupled Organization

Loosely coupled organization contrasts sharply with tightly coupled organization. Loosely coupled organizations have no center of authority, so they may appear to be disordered. Organization and personnel cooperation are possible without explicit design or procedures telling them what to do and when.[63]

---

[60]Diane Vaughan, The Challenger Launch Decision: Risky Technology, Culture, and Deviance at NASA (Chicago: University of Chicago Press, 1996), 415.

[61]Vernon Loeb, "CIA Chief Takes 'Responsibility' for Bombing of Chinese Embassy," *Washington Post*, 23 July 1999, A16; see also William M. Arkin, "Chinese Embassy Continues to Smolder," *Washington Post* (online version only), 8 November 1999, http://www.washingtonpost.com.

[62]George C. Tenet, "DCI Statement on the Belgrade Chinese Embassy Bombing." The DCI's statement is substantially the same as the formal statement issued by the State Department to the government of the People's Republic of China on 17 June 1999, http://www.usia.gov/regional/ea/uschina/bombrpt.htm, accessed 2000.

[63]Karl E. Weick, "Educational Organizations as Loosely Coupled Systems," *Administrative Science Quarterly* 21 (1976): 1–19.

A loosely coupled organization is not necessarily fragmented, i.e., in need of central direction; such organizations are a social and cognitive solution to constant environmental change.[64] Loosely coupled organizations have roles and task definitions that are not set by a single leader or authority. The components themselves set the tasks; there may be ambiguity in the application of particular technologies to accomplish some tasks; and participation in organizational activities is less determined by one's position on an organizational chart.[65] As a consequence, interaction and communication among components occur as needed and not as a result of commands or instructions. The roles of organizational components adjust on the basis of experience, and tasks are established by negotiation. The particular character of the matter at hand, rather than preset organizational arrangements, determines the components negotiating the tasks.[66]

Loosely coupled organizations have significant advantages over tightly coupled organizations in performing tasks in ambiguous or uncertain environments:[67]

1. Senior decision makers are less vulnerable to manipulation by information providers because links between in-

---

[64]Karl E. Weick, "Sources of Order in Underorganized Systems: Themes in Recent Organizational Theory," in *Organizational Theory and Inquiry*, ed. Yvonna S. Lincoln (Beverly Hills: Sage Publications, 1985), 131; Martin Landau, "On Multiorganizational Systems in Public Administration," *Journal of Public Administration Research and Theory* 1 (January 1991): 5-18.

[65]Weick notes that a "loosely coupled system is not a flawed system. It is a social and cognitive solution to constant environmental change." Weick, "Sources of Order in Underorganized Systems," 121.

[66]Landau, "On Multiorganizational Systems in Public Administration"; Weick, "Sources of Order in Underorganized Systems," 121.

[67]One obstacle to implementing loosely coupled organization in established formal organizations concerns the apportionment of credit (and reward) for successful performance. Instead of the senior leadership claiming credit for success (as occurs in tightly coupled hierarchies), the "team" assembled to deal with a particular task receives the credit. I am indebted to Jacob Neufeld for identifying this issue.

formation and its users are not specified clearly or rigidly.[68] However, accuracy of information remains a problem, regardless of whether it is compiled, entered into a database, and accessed on a weblike network with many contributors, or compiled and entered into a database by a single organizational component with a restricted set of users.

2. Such organizations are self-regulating because the stimuli for adaptation and innovation are the data generated by experience rather than by *a priori* demands of planners.[69]

3. Conscious employment of loosely coupled organization for uncertain or ambiguous tasks makes it easier for decision authority to flow to those best able to cope with the situation. Loose coupling avoids placing a calculational burden on central planners that, no matter how well supported by computers, cannot be achieved. Because novelty does not disrupt established routines very much, loosely coupled organizations are creative, adaptive, and open to innovation.[70]

---

[68]M. A. Feldman and James G. March, "Information in Organizations as Signal and Symbol," *Administrative Science Quarterly* 26 (1981): 171–186; Jacob A. Stockfisch, *Incentives and Information Quality in Defense Management*, R-1827-ARPA (Santa Monica, CA: RAND, 1976).

[69]See James A. Desveaux, *Designing Bureaucracies: Institutional Capacity and Large-Scale Problem-Solving* (Stanford, CA: Stanford University Press, 1995), 52.

[70]The adaptability of loosely coupled military organizations in wartime may offer a model for domestic agency programs, e.g., urban renewal or revitalization. Such programs need the ability to adapt quickly to a particular city's needs by identifying and creating links with appropriate city groups. James Q. Wilson cites Martha Derthick who noted that when Congress sets up new programs very quickly, it implicitly requires that agencies become capable of responding—"capable of devising new routines or altering new ones very quickly—[these qualities] are rarely found in large formal organizations." Wilson adds that "government agencies are far less flexible than formal organizations generally." During the Persian Gulf War, CENTCOM and CENTAF were very flexible, so flexible that a completely ad hoc organization provided C² for the air campaign. See James Q. Wilson, *Bureaucracy: What Government Agencies Do and Why They Do It* (New York: Basic Books, 1989), 368.

It appears that the introduction of carrier-based aviation into the Navy and the jet-propelled B-52 into the Air Force were accomplished by multiorganizational systems that had many features of loosely coupled systems.[71] The component organizations defined their tasks and set roles through mutual interaction. Senior decision makers were less vulnerable to the manipulation of information in their own component organizations, and the stimuli for adaptation and innovation were generated by real-world experience.

In wartime, significant portions of the military organizational structure below senior command often become less tightly coupled.[72] In this process, political scientist James Q. Wilson notes, uncertainty leads military organizations to transform themselves from agencies in which "outputs"—not "outcomes"—are measured to agencies in which outcomes but not outputs can be observed. Outputs are what subordinates do, e.g., fly some number of sorties each day; outcomes are the effects of organizational actions, e.g., defeat of a real enemy. The reason for the attention to outcomes of combat is simple: the "fog of war" and "friction" reduce the ability of senior leaders to observe what is happening on the battlefield.

During Operation Desert Storm, the ATO programmed significant portions of daily planning activities. Brig. Gen. Buster C. Glosson and Lt. Col. David A. Deptula chose from among the operational and organizational options available, using their conception of how airpower should be employed to identify appropriate options. The existence of some programmed activi-

[71]Mandeles, *The Development of the B-52 and Jet Propulsion*; Hone, Friedman, and Mandeles, *American and British Aircraft Carrier Development*.

[72]The impact of personality may be greater in loosely coupled organizations. The Black Hole was very different from normal military organizations in several important respects. For example, decision processes were informal because of the Black Hole planners' willingness to abandon previously established procedures and SOPs, and the lack of restraint on roles (Glosson was able to exercise influence well beyond his rank).

ties reduced the difficulty of pulling the whole enterprise to-gether. Problems and solutions could be prematched. But managing the entire CENTAF organization was still difficult. Hence, only a portion of the ATO entailed tight coupling of air operations, and these air operations primarily concerned targets in Iraq.

Many of the air operations over Kuwait were loosely cou-pled. Headquarters planning officers assigned aircraft to fly to particular geographical areas called "kill boxes." Once the fighter or attack aircraft were on location, officers on board EC-130E Airborne Battlefield Command and Control Center (ABCCC) aircraft and E-8A Joint Surveillance and Target At-tack Radar System (JSTARS) aircraft integrated battle informa-tion and issued directions to fighter and attack aircraft in near-real time. JSTARS aircraft, equipped with a moving target indi-cator and side-looking radar, could guide strike aircraft pre-cisely to moving vehicles. The ABCCC aircraft—essentially flying radio relay stations and command posts—also were able to forward battlefield information to strike aircraft, making it easier for pilots to find their designated targets. Together with E-3C Airborne Warning and Control System (AWACS) aircraft, JSTARS and ABCCC aircraft altered the organization of air combat in the direction of a more loosely coupled form as real and near-real time control of forces were exercised from the forward areas rather than the headquarters.

The Battle Control Center—a land-based version of the E-3 AWACS that is intended to replace a wing's operations com-mand post—tested this loosely coupled relationship among sur-veillance, sensor, and communications nodes in 1999. Center battle staffs were assigned particular territorial responsibilities for mobile targets and were buffered from central headquarters. The center was linked directly with E-8 JSTARS, satellites, the Predator and Global Hawk unmanned aerial vehicles, and sur-veillance aircraft. The test showed that aircraft could be directed to mobile ground targets not included in the ATO within thirty minutes, although this period is longer than the six minutes Iraqi mobile Scud teams took to fire their missiles and flee.[73] The Battle Control Center time lags between target identification and attack may be reduced by further improvements in organization and technology.[74]

Ground and sea forces in contact with the enemy are likely to adopt loosely coupled organization, as the increasing portability of precision navigation devices, satellite communications systems, and sensors allow U.S. forces to receive and process quickly the type of situational information formerly routed to a division.[75] As a result, U.S. forces may attack targets more efficiently. The end result of such operations should be increased lethality, higher tempo, and greater maneuverability. Table 6-2 summarizes the properties of loosely coupled organizations.

Features of Future Operations. Network-centric organization promises to increase the rate and accuracy of attacks against an adversary by employing the information-processing advantages of loosely coupled organization:

1. Roles and task definitions evolve in response to problems and without direction by a single leader or authority— the antithesis of military hierarchy.
2. The components themselves set the tasks. Interaction and

---

[73]The entire cycle of erecting the missiles, starting the launch sequences, firing the missiles, lowering the erector, packing, and leaving took less than one hour. H. Norman Schwarzkopf with Peter Petre, *It Doesn't Take a Hero* (New York: Bantom Books, 1992), 419; Defense Science Board, *Lessons Learned in Operations Desert Shield and Desert Storm*, 8 June 1992, 64–74.

[74]Bruce Rolfsen, "Joint Force Exercises Test U.S. Warfare Options," *Defense News* 14 (20 September 1999): 62.

[75]George I. Seffers, "U.S. Soldiers Put Personal Touch on New Technology," *Defense News* 13 (10 August 1998): 7.

TABLE 6-2.
Notional Structural Properties: Loosely Coupled Organization

Features	Properties
Coordination	• tasks are established by negotiation • parties to bargain (over tasks) are determined by the character of the issue • problems stimulate coordination efforts • roles are continuously adjusted by experience
Error Correction Strategies	• high redundancy • errors are more visible • independence of error correction efforts • some central direction is necessary to initiate action
Hierarchy	• the span at action level is wide • there are few organizational levels • tasks are less well-defined • many parallel paths lead to the top of the organization • there is a slight appearance of disorder
Potential Errors Generated by Structure	• a variant of the market problem—i.e., slowness to identify problem, slowness to act upon appearance of problem, and absence of centrally directed coordination to mesh activities across organizational levels—may arise • a bureaucratic entrepreneur may appear
Structure-Problem Match	• experimental modes for loosely coupled organization • measures of effectiveness replace measures of efficiency • loosely coupled organization is less rule-bound and more pragmatic • loosely coupled organization avoids placing great demands of calculation on a central planning mechanism • loosely coupled organization is less vulnerable to information manipulation

Implications of Loosely Coupled Organization for Coordination of Long-Range Precision Fires	• the theater combat commander coordinates with a specified commander to set and move fire-support coordination lines • the theater combat commander does not set long-range precision strike target sets or individual targets • the theater combat commander concentrates on coordinating U.S. combat forces engaging the enemy • a high operational tempo precludes senior civilian control of operations
C⁴ISR Technology Effects	• personnel at all organizational levels, including senior military leaders, operate at a higher tempo as they take on more tasks • organizational complexity increases as the number of occupational specialties increases; the need for increased numbers of personnel grows • coordination is more difficult • multiple information and communications channels provide senior leaders with higher capability to attack the enemy's decision-making process but less direct control of own forces; subordinate leaders have greater discretion • the danger of uncertainty absorption is ever present as information is directed to senior leaders • informal organizations are more important to operation's success

communication among components occur as needed and not as a result of commands or instructions.

3. Organizational roles of components adjust on the basis of experience, and tasks are established by negotiation.

During Operation Allied Force, for example, the pilot of an F-117 fighter returning from a mission saw Yugoslav MiG fighters on their runway. The pilot's observation was transmitted from the Balkans to U.S. land-based information-processing sites, then to the Navy's Tomahawk mission planning facility in Norfolk, which forwarded the MiG's coordinates to a specific ship for the missile launch. The time elapsed between the transmission of the MiG's location and the Tomahawk missile strike was only 101 minutes.[76] The details of this Tomahawk strike are reminiscent of an informal network created during Operation Desert Storm by a naval joint staff officer to provide the GAT with satellite-based BDA of targets only forty-five minutes after a Tomahawk missile attack.[77] In both cases, the components—rather than headquarters—set the tasks on the basis of need and adjusted their activities on the basis of experience.

A key organizational problem for military planners, despite these clear advantages of loose coupling, is the distributed decision making of loosely coupled and network-centric organization, which undercuts authority in current military organization, wherein rank symbolizes authority. Advocates of C⁴ISR systems promise greater control of forces over wider operations, but the environment and organization must be stable for such control to operate. That is, the observation of predicted environments or solutions must trigger the engagement of previously created SOPs. The creation of an SOP for combat is not as simple as flipping a hamburger at McDonald's, where the range of potential environments is much smaller. In combat, the range of SOPs suitable to respond to an adversary's actions must be wide to accommodate possible surprises. The necessity of creating many SOPs as possible responses to potential adversary actions reduces leadership attention to the specifics and timing of matching each combat task to a previously devised

[76]Robert Holzer, "Report: U.S. Navy Used Arms Effectively in Kosovo," *Defense News* 14 (30 August 1999): 6.

[77]Mandeles, Hone, and Terry, *Managing "Command and Control,"* 21, 39.

SOP; combat leadership becomes less important than the creation of the SOPs. Assuming a large and coherent set of SOPs
matching likely military environments can be created (and that
these SOPs will remain valid over time or be replaced in a
timely manner when needed, i.e., before combat), the primary
job for military leaders becomes searching through the SOPs to
find an appropriate match for a combat task. But all is not well
with this scenario because no matter how well prepared with
automated tools, such as search engines, the task of rummaging
through myriad SOPs will tax the computational abilities of
military leaders already operating under the stress of combat.

A second organizational problem for military planners concerns the "structural context" created by loose coupling of sub-
components or offices. The relative absence of central direction
and the time and effort required for effective negotiation and
mutual adjustment may reduce capacity of personnel to consider operational- or strategic-level goals. Persons in relatively
compartmented offices may pursue goals or policies that unintentionally produce problems for people in other offices. Such
a situation provides an opportunity for the appearance of a bureaucratic entrepreneur, who centralizes functions to act more
effectively, especially to ensure the completion of time-sensitive
tasks.[78] However, the entrepreneur may guarantee timely decisions by reducing the quality of analysis or ignoring information inconsistent with preconceived notions. In following the
lead of a bureaucratic entrepreneur, organizational members
may easily become fixated on suboptimal resource allocations,
strategies, or technologies, or overreact to "noise" or distraction. Taken together, these actions may foreclose the experi-

[78]For example, Eugene Lewis, *Public Entrepreneurship: Toward a Theory of Bureaucratic Political Power* (Bloomington: Indiana University Press, 1980); Martin Levin
and Barbara Ferman, "The Political Hand: Policy Implementation and Youth Employment Programs," *Journal of Policy Analysis and Management* 5 (Winter 1986):
311–325.

mentation necessary for discovering good alternatives. This type of false learning can lead to further actions that compound error rather than correct it. Hence, loosely coupled organizations may create the very conditions that invalidate their theoretical information-processing advantages for decision making under uncertainty and ambiguity. Furthermore, in ambiguous environments, the energetic and opportunistic individual has greater opportunity to affect the direction and interplay of actions.[79]

Early in Operation Desert Shield, for example, Brig. Gen. Buster C. Glosson discovered that the compartmentalization of intelligence functions prevented the accomplishment of critical planning tasks and reduced the senior leaders' situational awareness. The CENTAF manner of planning an air campaign resulted in the over-elaboration of different functions and specializations, leading to fragmentation and ineffective planning. Indeed, CENTAF was overwhelmed by many tasks in the days immediately following the Iraqi invasion of Kuwait. In response, Glosson saw a need to tie together intelligence gathering and analysis agencies in the continental United States to air campaign planners in Riyadh and indirectly to the units in the field. Glosson thereby circumvented the established intelligence organization and SOPs—ostensibly designed to provide high-quality information and analysis—and created his own ad hoc intelligence channels to provide campaign planners with information on his desired schedule.

Glosson's efforts to acquire timely and useful target and BDA intelligence had cascading implications for the effective management of the air campaign. As noted in chapter 4, Glosson's willingness to order last-minute changes to the ATO in-

---

[79]Fred I. Greenstein, "The Impact of Personality on Politics: An Attempt to Clear Away Underbrush," *American Political Science Review* 61 (September 1967): 629–641; Sidney Hook, *The Hero in History: A Study in Limitation and Possibility* (New Brunswick, NJ: Transaction Publishers, 1992).

duced a positive feedback cycle of target change orders that
made the planning process unstable and reduced "situation
awareness." Last-minute changes complicated, and in many
cases made impossible, the process of BDA. Mid-level officers
recognized the need to moderate the target-change orders. By
appointing a "Buster Control Officer," they also developed an
ad hoc and informal method to improve the planning process
by reducing the number of last-minute changes.[80] Because of
the operational tempo and pressure of wartime decision making, Glosson's own ad hoc organization—the GAT cell—could
not easily calculate and compare the benefits and costs of its
usurpation of functions performed elsewhere in CENTAF (nor
was anyone disposed to ask the question). Hence, organizations
are not necessarily protected from failure by loose coupling because these qualities can change when people ignore data, cen-
tralize authority, or are subjected to stress.

News Media Organization

A third notional organizational structure that may potentially
be applied to future military operations, a news media organization, combines some features of both loosely and tightly coupled organization. News media organizations employ three
overlapping principles to organize information processing.
First, there is a territorial division of news gathering.[81] Meta-
phorically, a picture of the nodes and locations of entities gathering news is like a spider's web; the central office branches out
to connect with bureaus and news beats and joins with other
diverse news media.[82] Second, news media may divide the world

[80]Mandeles, Hone, and Terry, *Managing "Command and Control,"* 48–49.
[81]Gaye Tuchman, *Making News: A Study in the Construction of Reality* (New York: Free Press, 1978), 25.
[82]Ibid., 20.

by topical specialization. Independent departments have their own budgets, and their editors bypass the territorial desks, reporting directly to a managing or executive editor.[83] Third, superimposed over the territorial and topical divisions of news collection is the problem of deadlines; decisions about what goes into a newspaper or a radio or television newscast have to be made before a printing or air deadline.[84]

The concepts used to classify news stories—spot news (events unscheduled by the newsroom, e.g., a murder), soft news ("human interest" stories, e.g., scams committed against the gullible elderly), continuing news (stories defined by subject matter, e.g., the movement of legislation through Congress), hard news (factual presentations of events that may be subject to analysis or interpretation, e.g., election results), and developing news (a combination of spot and hard news, e.g., an earthquake)—were created to respond to publishing deadlines rather than to anything substantive about the resulting story or the characteristics of the event covered.[85] These five categories do not closely represent what is happening in the world, nor do they represent what the final story will look like. The categories simply mirror the administrative and management problem of scheduling the work created by the story.[86]

In addition to using schedules to organize information processing, newsrooms employ hierarchical and other means to coordinate and direct the work. Frequently, one person or group of people—the heads of territorial desks and of specialized topical departments—is assigned responsibility for knowing what is being captured in the news net. Above them, the managing or executive editor coordinates their tasks. At mid

---

[83]Ibid., 29.
[84]Ibid., 45.
[85]Ibid., 47.
[86]Ibid., 48.

levels of the newsroom hierarchy, some coordination occurs by self-organization—the reporters coordinate their activities with minimal direction from above. City rooms often are large, with no partitions between desks, permitting reporters to track each other's activities, and an editor to scan the room quickly to see who is available for assignment.

Scheduling and coordinating works by coding news events according to the five categories structures but does not maintain tight control of work. Direct supervision of the work process rather than the product—the story—would require an expensive organizational investment in more editorial personnel. To avoid this type of organization and expenditure, news organizations encourage "professionalism" among reporters, who know how to get a story that meets organizational needs and standards. This reliance on professionalism also means every reporter must be, to some extent, a generalist who is able to do others' work. The mutual and widespread knowledge of tasks and roles allows reporters to negotiate overlapping lines of territorial, institutional, and topical responsibilities.[87]

A news organization, as a complex bureaucracy, can develop general rules to assign tasking authority in many situations of overlapping responsibility. However, it cannot anticipate all possible problems of deciding how to gather and process information from a news event. Hence, news organizations do not try to devise rules for all possible news events because rigid delineation of responsibility may prevent the organization from acting upon unanticipated situations and problems.

As in military organizations, news organizations have had to adapt to higher operating tempos resulting from new computer, information-processing, and communications technologies. Editors have found that computers have created new opportunities (1) to use graphics to illustrate stories, (2) to con-

---

[87]Ibid., 65–66.

trol the design and content of newspaper pages, (3) to share information and rewrite stories, and (4) to speed research. The introduction of new information-processing technologies and the use of satellite communications have speeded the process of news gathering and story transmission from one location to another. Although they affect how the work is done, the new technologies have not altered the logic of how deadlines affect work schedules.[88] Table 6-3 summarizes the properties of media organizations.

Features of Future Operations. The newsroom offers some interesting analogies for military organizations. First, future military organizations organized along the lines of a newsroom would assign territorial or theater responsibility to particular senior commanders and create a division of labor and classify operations by deadlines to (1) synchronize information gathering about friendly and enemy forces, (2) assign targets or actions, (3) transmit orders, (4) apply fires, and (5) receive and integrate BDAs. Some functions might overlap among theater and unified commands and require centralized direction, e.g., the employment of nuclear weapons or intercontinental ballistic missile precision strikes against valuable targets. On the one hand, the segregation of such functions from the theater command would require dedicated coordination to eliminate the possibility of friendly fire mishaps or conflicts similar to the establishment of fire-support coordination lines.[89] Some informal organizations, however, make the formal organization more reliable and robust, e.g., the operation of informal groups that ensure reliable flight operations on U.S. aircraft carriers. On the

---

[88]Society for News Design and American Society of Newspaper Editors, *Technology and Pagination: Integrating the* New *into Your Newsroom* (Providence, RI: Society for News Design, 1999).

[89]Robert J. D'Amico, "Joint Fires Coordination: Service Competencies and Boundary Challenges," *Joint Force Quarterly* (Spring 1999): 70–77.

TABLE 6-3.

Notional Structural Properties: News Media Organization

Features	*Properties*
Coordination	• small groups of coordinators guide the action • the work of personnel in separate territorial and topical components is coordinated through interaction and discussion • coordinators exist at multiple organizational levels
Error Correction Strategies	• efforts are frequently duplicated across the industry—in other words, news organizations copy each other's stories and actions; this can either widely diffuse errors or ensure accuracy • negotiation within each news organization determines the response to a news event • management and personnel accept the elusiveness of truth
Hierarchy	• tasks are moderately well-defined • there are few organizational levels • the span at the action level is wide • the action level is defined topically and territorially
Potential Errors Generated by Structure	• multiple media organizations will copy each other and make the same mistakes • communications and information-processing technologies may increase personnel tempos and individual-level stress • communications and information-processing technologies may ease the difficulty of doing some types of research but may also magnify the potential for quickly publishing errors • work tempos may differ according to one's location in the organization, creating difficulties in coding events, gathering information, and finding people not otherwise engaged to do emergency tasks

Structure-Problem Match	• temporal classification of news events permits managers to cope with work-flow and assign organizational resources • moderate delineation of roles allows response to unanticipated problems
Implications of News Media Organization Analogy for Coordination of Long-Range Precision Fires	• one organizational component is dedicated to long-range fires • higher personnel and operational tempos can degrade effectiveness • advanced communications and information-processing technology does not necessarily lead to greater operational capability
C⁴ISR Technology Effects	• personnel and operational tempos increase • organizational complexity increases • temporal deadlines continue to be more important than accuracy of individual story components

other hand, the segregation of some functions from the theater command should help conserve the attention and decision-making resources of theater commanders so that they may concentrate on the unfolding battle.

Second, future military organizations might have dedicated cores of generalists and specialists interspersed throughout the organization to complement each other's perspectives. Senior command would not be reserved for either a specialist or generalist. In media organizations, occupational specialties are ignored when necessary; everyone must be capable of doing everyone else's work. This situation, too, has a counterpart aboard warships; personnel have many collateral duties. The proliferation of collateral duties is necessary because of warship space limitations, but it also imposes severe personnel tempo strains during deployments. In combat, the proliferation of collateral duties may reduce operational effectiveness as some tasks may be delayed in emergency situations, e.g., in a trade-off among firefighting, damage-control, and flight-deck operations. The current effort of engineers to design ships to operate with small crews risks operational failures as the number of collateral duties assigned to individuals increases.

Third, the new communications and information-processing technologies create new staffing problems for media organizations: there is more work for fewer people, and training to use the new technologies has been inadequate. Similarly, C⁴ISR technologies will create new staffing problems for future military organizations as personnel try to do more tasks in shorter periods. In addition to staffing problems for news media and military organizations, the new information-processing and communications technologies create the need to develop new means to identify and mitigate errors. For the news media, the increased speed in transmitting stories great distances or in formatting a story for radio, television, or the print media does nothing to ensure the clarity of a story or a story's factual descriptive accuracy.[90] The same relationship between transmission speed and accuracy obtains for military organizations, where the speedy transmission of false, ambiguous, or irrelevant information does not enhance operational effectiveness.

Some features of newsroom operations also seem inappropriate for a military organization. First, the wire services and news net substantively duplicate one another's efforts, e.g., news media send reporters to occurrences they learned about through wire-service accounts. In other words, media organizations "borrow" stories from one another, and reporters share information. This situation provides an opportunity for manipulation of the "news" by public relations firm operatives (an analogue of the efforts by adversary disinformation or psyops

[90]Lewis D. Dolinsky, Deputy Foreign Editor, *San Francisco Chronicle*, interview with author, 11 October 1999.

groups). The ultimate effect of duplication of effort is that the news media and the news services leave the same holes in the news. Such copying of errors is undesirable for military leaders, for whom inadequate situational awareness of enemy and their own forces incurs severe costs.

Informal Organization

It is trivial to observe that to accomplish their missions, military organizations must process a large volume of information and operate with a great deal of knowledge about their own forces, the environment, and adversary forces. The need to respond to operational problems not anticipated—or exacerbated—by formal organizational structure makes informal and ad hoc organizational arrangements critically important in identifying, suppressing, and mitigating errors.[91] The structure and incentives embedded in some formal organizational designs, e.g., tightly coupled organizations in authoritarian regimes, may encourage informal groups to behave in ways that impair the long-term solution of organizational problems.[92]

The aircraft carrier is a good example of how informal groups and the tacit knowledge that supports them ensure organizational reliability and effective performance of tightly coupled complex technologies (e.g., nuclear reactors for propulsion

---

[91]See for example Victor A. Thompson, *Organizations as Systems* (Morristown, NJ: General Learning Press, 1973), 9; Jennifer J. Halpern, "Cognitive Factors Influencing Decision Making in a Highly Reliable Organization," *Industrial Crisis Quarterly* 3 (1989): 143–158; Karl E. Weick, "Mental Models of High Reliability Systems," *Industrial Crisis Quarterly* 3 (1989): 127–142; John R. Harrald, Ruth Cohn, and William A. Wallace, " 'We Were Always Re-Organizing . . .': Some Crisis Management Implications of the *Exxon Valdez* Oil Spill," *Industrial Crisis Quarterly* 6 (1992): 197–217.

[92]For example, Joseph S. Berliner observed that the Soviet means of rationing supply by central planning led to hoarding (and black marketeering) by factory managers, thus further disrupting the distribution of resources in the Soviet economy. Berliner, *The Factory Manager in the USSR* (Cambridge: Harvard University Press, 1957).

and jet aircraft).[93] Aircraft carriers are formally organized by rank, but critical aspects of flight operations are monitored closely by the many informal networks that cut across the formal hierarchy and the many lateral adaptations that ensure tasks are completed. Gene I. Rochlin, a member of a team of university analysts investigating aircraft carriers as "high reliability organizations," observed:

> When these [informal] networks activate, they intervene via a process of ongoing and continuing arguments and negotiations among personnel from many units in person and via phone, which tend to be resolved by direct order only when the rare impasse develops that requires an appeal to higher authority.[94]

These informal networks are a means for the incorporation of "tacit knowledge"[95]—empirical, experiential knowledge gained through practice or "on the job training"—into the formal organization. Tacit knowledge plays a large role in flight operations. No one in the Navy can specify and sequence every task that needs to be performed to get aircraft off the flight deck.[96] Yet, the aircraft do fly and accidents are rare.

There are three distinct organizations in the carrier: the internal structures of the ship, the air wing, and the battle group.

---

[93]Karl E. Weick and Karlene H. Roberts, "Collective Mind in Organizations: Heedful Interrelating on Flight Decks," in *Organizational Learning*, eds. Michael D. Cohen and Lee S. Sproull (Thousand Oaks, CA: Sage Publications, 1996), 353.

[94]Gene I. Rochlin, "Informal Organizational Networks as a Crisis-Avoidance Strategy: US Naval Flight Operations as a Case Study," *Industrial Crisis Quarterly* 3 (1989): 167.

[95]See for example Michael Polanyi, *Personal Knowledge: Towards a Post-Critical Philosophy* (Chicago: University of Chicago Press, 1974).

[96]The author's discussions with naval officers aboard USS *George Washington*, 30–31 October 1999; Rochlin, "Informal Organizational Networks as a Crisis-Avoidance Strategy," 164.

Naval flight operations cause a level of organizational complexity not present in land-based flight operations because of interactions that link and span these three organizations:[97] the different quasi-permanent informal networks responsible for the carrier's primary tasks, including engineering, navigation, air operations, flight- and hangar-deck control, and strike planning; and the informal problem-solving networks that are activated when operations appear to present danger or errors. In flight operations, rank and deference give way to experience and problem-solving ability when these informal networks are active.[98] Indeed, the networks are exercised and drilled as part of the training process that continues throughout the deployment.[99] Once the immediate danger ends, rank ensures that the networks disappear when no longer needed.

Naval flight operations are an outcome of a particular form of organization—"high reliability organizations"—that continuously operates safely under hazardous conditions.[100] They require adaptation "to time-urgent demands under contingencies and circumstances that are hard to plan and impossible to anticipate, under conditions of high but unknown risk, severe potential consequence, high technical complexity (both in so-

---

[97]Rochlin, "Informal Organizational Networks as a Crisis-Avoidance Strategy," 163.

[98]Halpern, "Cognitive Factors Influencing Decision Making in a Highly Reliable Organization."

[99]Rochlin, "Informal Organizational Networks as a Crisis-Avoidance Strategy," 168; Lt. David Peach, interview with the author, USS *George Washington*, 30 October 1999.

[100]Roberts, "New Challenges in Organizational Research"; Weick and Roberts, "Collective Mind in Organizations"; Gene I. Rochlin, "'High-Reliability' Organizations and Technical Change: Some Ethical Problems and Dilemmas," *IEEE Technology and Society Magazine*, September 1986, 3–9; Gene I. Rochlin, Todd R. LaPorte, and Karlene H. Roberts, "The Self-Designing High Reliability Organization: Aircraft Carrier Flight Operations at Sea," *Naval War College Review* 40 (Autumn 1987), 76–90; Todd R. LaPorte, Karlene Roberts, and Gene I. Rochlin, "High Reliability Organizations: The Research Challenge," (Institute of Governmental Studies, University of California, Berkeley, December 1987).

phistication and in the coupling between the various units and elements), and very tight organizational coupling."[101] Key factors in these highly reliable operations are the presence of many "informal, problem-specific organizational networks that have been self-designed and self-implemented" and the transmission of "lessons" to younger crewmembers and to the crews of other ships.[102] Individuals, since they are assigned and drilled in several collateral duties, perform a variety of roles in informal networks depending upon the presence or nature of a problem or crisis. When an operational problem occurs, rank is irrelevant to discovering a solution—i.e., the expertise of low-ranking persons is not discounted.[103]

The shipboard informal networks, unlike other informal groups discussed in organizational theory literature, do not become formalized over time. They appear when problem-solving knowledge is required and disappear when the problem has been solved.[104] In high reliability organizations, people avoid being overloaded with information by knowing what they are looking for. They know what to look for because of continuous training and discussions among themselves.[105]

Tightly coupled organizations assume that errors will be readily detected because nearly perfect knowledge of the system is possible. But this assumption is not tenable for complex, tightly coupled person-machine-organization systems, given the growing burden of requiring comprehensive, timely knowledge of state and process. Complete state and process knowl-

---

[101]Rochlin, "Informal Organizational Networks as a Crisis-Avoidance Strategy," 163.

[102]Information on self-designed and implemented networks is from Rochlin, "Informal Organizational Networks as a Crisis-Avoidance Strategy," 161. Information on the lessons of younger crewmembers is from the author's discussions with naval officers aboard USS *George Washington*, 30–31 October 1999.

[103]Roberts, "New Challenges in Organizational Research," 9.

[104]Rochlin, "Informal Organizational Networks as a Crisis-Avoidance Strategy," 161.

[105]The author's discussions with naval officers aboard USS *George Washington*, 30–31 October 1999; Roberts, "New Challenges in Organizational Research," 9.

edge at the required level is not achievable. "Expertise" of human operators using tacit knowledge must replace analytical models. Personnel training must be designed to create generalized experiential knowledge or expertise, i.e., the capability to act when one does not employ a fully specified model.

In flight operations, supervisors and operators are wary of the overuse of predictive, programmed analytical models. They believe that the range of possible errors and hazards is so wide that it defeats the design of a "better or more comprehensive operating model."[106] The uncertainties in flight operations belong to the set of problems engineers call "unknown unknowns." On aircraft carriers, responding to unknown unknowns is a self-designed process "in which adaptive modes and structures for redundant monitoring of operations and flexible crisis intervention and response are created within and by the operating organization to deal with the recognized range and variance of contingencies and errors that they have observed."[107] High-reliability organizations can employ peaked hierarchy and tight coordination of activities because these organizational forms have redundant means of calculation and potential command embodied in a "flexible set of ad hoc and informal networks."[108] Similarly, networks of ad hoc and informal organizations saved the formal organization of CENTAF during the Persian Gulf War.[109] Such networks also obtain in ground combat, as shown by the Marine Corps's Urban Warrior experiments, which explore battlefield advantages of informal organization.[110]

---

[106]Rochlin, "Informal Organizational Networks as a Crisis-Avoidance Strategy," 165.

[107]Ibid., 165.

[108]Roberts, "New Challenges in Organizational Research," 10.

[109]Mandeles, Hone, and Terry, Managing "Command and Control," chap. 3.

[110]Joel Garreau, "Reboot Camp: As War Looms, the Marines Test New Networks of Comrades," Washington Post, 24 March 1999, C1.

Conclusion

The transformation of U.S. military forces into organizations heavily dependent on computer-based information processing and satellite communications already has had several effects: the organizational complexity of combat organizations has increased, combat organizations are more dependent on continental U.S.–based support organizations, and command of forces has become more difficult. There is no systematic knowledge about how people and organizations operating complex and hazardous technologies may perform more effectively, and a concerted program of experimentation and analysis to gain that type of knowledge remains undeveloped. A significant portion of such a program must focus on investigating and tracing implications of organizational design for combat effectiveness.

This chapter explored situations in which tightly coupled, loosely coupled, and news media organizational structures are appropriate to combat. At an operational level, the effective conduct of long-range precision strike operations requires extensive cause-effect knowledge that clearly relates actions (e.g., the physical destruction or functional degradation of target sets) to outcomes (e.g., military incapacity or political surrender). At a tactical level, tightly coupled organizations function well when complemented by trained and motivated individuals working together in ad hoc or informal organizations. For those military tasks that are not supported as extensively by clear causal knowledge, a loosely coupled organizational structure and associated technologies are more appropriate to the rapidly changing conditions, ambiguity, and uncertainty of combat. Combat operations by loosely coupled organizations will require more conscious employment of informal organizations to identify and mitigate error, which will entail changes in (1) training and recruitment of personnel at all organizational levels, (2) the conduct of C^2, and (3) how the national security community learns to conduct combat operations more effectively. The final chapter will tie together the various threads of analysis in the preceding chapters and discuss a strategy to transform the current military into a mid-twenty-first-century force.

CHAPTER 7

A Military Revolution by the Mid-Twenty-First Century

Mistakes are systematic and socially organized, built into the nature of professions, organizations, cultures, and structures.[1]

P eople employing late-twentieth-century technologies, including computer, communications, and sensor equipment, are transforming existing military organizational relationships and structures. No one can fully predict the organizational and operational outcomes of frequently "upgrading" existing or introducing new C⁴ISR equipment and software into combat organizations. Nor are the features of proposed operational concepts, e.g., "information superiority," well understood.

The national security community does not approach questions about how to develop and support an RMA with a widely accepted analytical framework. Lacking adequate models that relate technological and organizational changes with individual-level cognitive and knowledge requirements, military leaders can't predict the effects of changes to information levels or information asymmetries on combat operations.[2] Yet, trying to

---

[1]Diane Vaughan, *The Challenger Launch Decision: Risky Technology, Culture, and Deviance at NASA* (Chicago: University of Chicago Press, 1996), 415.

[2]For example, a June 1999 Defense Science Board task force argued that inadequate use of modeling and simulation tools might stunt innovation on future battlefields. Models and simulation tools do not include critical features of Joint Vision 2010 operational concepts or the emerging security environment. David Mulholland, "Panel Finds JV2010 Needs More Models," *Defense News* 14 (5 July 1999): 22, 26.

anticipate the operational and organizational implications of the C⁴ISR acquisition path is important because, as Congressman William Nichols noted in reviewing the 1986 legislation to reorganize the DOD, organizations are weapons of war.[3]

New C⁴ISR technologies will generate new capabilities—but higher technical performance is not necessarily equivalent to higher operational capability. During World War II, for example, British radars proved technologically less capable than the German *Freya* and *Wurzberg* systems. The British system, however, uniquely linked radars, observers, pilots, and staff in the operations room. This combination of personnel and machines gave the British an operational advantage. The integrated data allowed British personnel to distinguish their own forces from "bogies" (unidentified aircraft) and "bandits" (enemy aircraft). With every bogie and bandit assigned to a sector, the sector controller then assigned aircraft to meet the enemy.[4]

In an effort to elucidate longer-term systemic and societal implications of new military C⁴ISR technologies, previous chapters have addressed a wide spectrum of topics: inferences and levels of analysis, past efforts to understand and adapt to unfolding military revolutions, combat forces C², the network-centric warfare concept, the conduct of air campaigns against Iraq and Kosovo, organizational design, and informal organizations. The range of these topics is different from what one might expect to read in a standard systems analysis.[5] The purpose of this research effort has been to emulate the type of analysis Bernard Brodie produced: an investigation of the kind of

---

[3] William Nichols, "Opening Statement," *Hearings before the Investigation Subcommittee of the Committee on Armed Services*, House of Representatives, 99th Cong., 2nd sess., 19 February 1986, 3.

[4] See Peter Townsend, *Duel of Eagles* (New York: Pocket Books, 1972), 275; Thomas P. Coakley, *Command and Control for War and Peace* (Washington, DC: NDU Press, 1992), 30.

[5] Bernard Brodie, "Technology, Politics, and Strategy," in *Problems of Modern Strategy* (New York: Praeger, 1970), 160, 169.

analysis that should be done and an examination of questions hidden by numbers on a briefing chart. It remains to tie together the themes underlying these topics and to apply that understanding to combat in the twenty-first century.

The Role of Institutions and Organizations

Through institutions and organizations, people impose structure on their interactions to reduce uncertainty about each other's behavior. Not all institutional or organizational structures are effective in planning and conducting military operations. A review of the last one hundred years of military history reveals only a few American military organizations capable of creating RMA-type equipment or operational concepts (e.g., carrier-based aviation; the swept-wing, long-range, jet-propelled B-52; the fleet ballistic missile; and Lockheed's "skunk works"[6]). Creating such an organization to ready the entire U.S. military for the mid-twenty-first century will, therefore, not be easy. One might well ask: How does one account for the uneven and erratic pattern of military innovation that led to past qualitative improvements in operational capability? How should military organizations model future processes of development and change?

Some conditions accompany successful American-style RMA organizations. The U.S. Constitution provides institutional rules (e.g., separation of powers and checks and balances) that permit wide access to the decision-making process and the

[6]For more on RMA-type equipment and concepts see Thomas C. Hone, Norman Friedman, and Mark D. Mandeles, *American and British Aircraft Carrier Development, 1919–1941* (Annapolis, MD: Naval Institute Press, 1999); Mark D. Mandeles, *The Development of the B-52 and Jet Propulsion* (Maxwell AFB, AL: Air University Press, 1998); Harvey M. Sapolsky, *The Polaris System Development* (Cambridge: Harvard University Press, 1972); and Ben R. Rich and Leo Janos, *Skunk Works* (Boston: Little, Brown, 1994).

formation of multiorganizational systems—interacting and overlapping associations of organizations.[7] The interaction among agencies in multiorganizational systems is self-correcting; personnel at all levels learn about problems and help devise solutions. Yet, there is significant variation in the self-correcting ability of different multiorganizational systems—some do it better than others. The absence or presence of additional organizational-level variables—e.g., the application of the rules of evidence and inference to evaluate history and experiments—are critical to system performance.[8]

Philosopher Israel Scheffler observed that "familiarity—in life—may breed contempt. In thought, it typically breeds complacency and misunderstanding."[9] Likewise, familiarity with organizations in daily life hides organizational problems, fostering a false sense of clarity about the multilevel interactions that accompany large-scale acquisition of technologies. Inventing new forms of organization to complement new types of operations entails fundamental problems of, first, providing sufficient resources to the innovating elite and, second, recruiting, maintaining, motivating, and organizing people in a structure that will function continuously. The second problem evokes the most concern, especially regarding (1) the far-reaching effects of ever more advanced C^{4}ISR technologies on specialization of organizational roles, (2) the highly technical and wide-ranging skills required of RMA officers, (3) increasingly complex information flows within organizations, and (4) the development of ad hoc and informal organization as a means to mitigate unanticipated flaws of the formal organization.

---

[7]Martin Landau, "On Multiorganizational Systems in Public Administration," *Journal of Public Administration Research and Theory* 1 (January 1991): 5–18.

[8]During the interwar period, the Navy's General Board paid close attention to the problem of what evidence would be appropriate to support particular aircraft or ship designs. See Hone, Friedman, and Mandeles, *American and British Aircraft Carrier Development, 1919–1941.*

[9]Israel Scheffler, *Inquiries* (Indianapolis, IN: Hackett Publishing, 1986), 338.

Organizational Size and Specialization of Occupational Roles.
A discussion of organizational size must examine such factors as (1) coordination of people and their specialized roles, (2) the "transaction" costs of transmitting and processing information and instructions, (3) various organizational obstacles to analysis (e.g., premature programming and self-delusion), and (4) person-machine-organization interactions. Political efforts to reduce the size of the military are partly designed to reduce the number and cost of errors from each of the above factors. However, reducing the size of the military will not, in fact, reduce such errors and may even increase them.

The complexity of operating advanced C^{4}ISR networked systems creates the need for ever more specialized organizational and occupational roles. However, the movement toward smaller force structures (in all Western militaries) hinders the appropriate specialization to perform tasks. The RMA will reverse the movement toward decreasing the numbers of people in the military services because the larger numbers of specialized occupational positions to operate specialized equipment pose a need for coordination, requiring larger numbers of people to supervise and integrate the work of the many specialists. The knowledge burden imposed on personnel by advanced C^{4}ISR equipment will not allow a force composed of generalists capable of performing a wide range of collateral tasks.

In addition to increasing the difficulty of coordinating forces and countering the trend toward smaller militaries, specialization will affect what experiences are necessary for command. The organizational importance of network administrators increases as complex C^{4}ISR equipment and software become ever more essential to the operational delivery of munitions. Thus, the inevitable rise of the network administrator will generate significant new organizational conflict and associated questions about promotion pathways and experience necessary for command. Continuing to acquire complex C^{4}ISR equipment while attempting to reduce personnel numbers will complicate the transformation of a future RMA force. The question facing senior leaders is not: will C⁴ISR technologies mandate greater specialization? Rather, the questions facing them are: how will the inevitable specialization of roles and tasks be organized, and how will leaders organize to evaluate and refine the organization?

The RMA Officer. Organizational power is a short-run asset, but a long-term liability.[10] Power allows an organization to change its environment rather than adapt to it. An organization's ability to define an environment, in which it can organize to achieve a specific plan without concern about contingencies, provides an advantage. In the long-run, however, the ability to determine portions of the peacetime political environment may atrophy the ability to respond to change on the battlefield.

Chapter 5 reviewed the significant cognitive demands on memory, calculation, and coordination that will be placed on personnel at all levels of a network-centric combat command during operations. Such cognitive demands necessitate a concerted effort to create organizations staffed by personnel who will respond to change rather than impose a plan. Dedicating resources to develop RMA "renaissance man" officers and noncommissioned officers, specifically trained to be interdisciplinary, will appropriately combat these demands. The purpose of this educational effort should be to create a class of personnel whose knowledge is not specialized to current technologies and markets but rather is wide-ranging and deep. Training to acquire wide-ranging and deep knowledge may not have immedi-

---

[10]James G. March, with Chip Heath, *A Primer on Decision Making: How Decisions Happen* (New York: Free Press, 1994), 248; Karl W. Deutsch, *The Nerves of Government: Models of Political Communication and Control* (New York: Free Press, 1966), 111.

ate pay-offs, but it results in a greater ability to adapt to uncertainty and ambiguity in battle and to changes in the security environment. In addition, such RMA personnel will be highly valued in both civilian and military organizations.

However, daily activities impose constraints on the military's ability to train and develop RMA personnel. The high knowledge burden that increasingly complex technologies and short deadlines of combat operations place on individuals is actually exacerbated by frequent rotation of military personnel—a policy that provides soldiers with general experience and background for higher positions. The demanding knowledge requirements of network-centric operations militate against using many short-duration assignments to gain the appropriate tacit knowledge. Training the RMA officer and noncommissioned officer to act flexibly will be an expensive and on-going enterprise. The knowledge-burden problem is only part of a critical set of interrelated personnel and recruitment issues, such as:

1. The military will have to compete against civilian employers for persons having required skills or high capacity to learn those skills. Those individuals who have the native intelligence, preservice education and training, and service training to perform in a network-centric military organization will become very attractive for many kinds of high-paying civilian positions. One way to avoid competing against the civilian economy for talented personnel is to institute a type of "revolving door" national service personnel policy, which would substitute a set of short-term assignments for a long-term commitment.[11] This policy would be applied to only critical technical fields; applied widely, the revolving door national service

---

[11] I am indebted to Thomas C. Hone for this insight.

policy would duplicate the problems of frequent rotation. In addition to financial rewards, the military services will have to offer status incentives to enter and remain in service, promoting the rewards of public service, the challenges of operating in an elite occupation, and high adventure.

2. The future personality profile of persons who desire to serve in RMA military organizations is likely to change.[12] In the past, many military occupational specialties were well suited to those who prefer the discipline of solving well-defined problems and fulfilling clear organizational roles and who have a lower tolerance for uncertainty and ambiguity. A completely different mindset and personality profile may be required to operate effectively within a C⁴ISR-type force. Interaction in such organizations will require personnel more comfortable with higher levels of uncertainty and ambiguity and who have highly developed skills in negotiation and coordination.

3. As C⁴ISR technology matures and new operational concepts emerge, RMA personnel will become conscious of their distinctively new way of conducting warfare, as well as their collective needs and interests. Similarly, a wide range of new roles and civilian organizations may co-evolve with further development of C⁴ISR technology

[12]Jean de Bloch frequently noted that future warfare would require officers to have different intellectual habits:

> Even the courage which down to a short time ago was the open sesame to military success has become a drawback rather than an advantage. Prudence, initiative, independence have taken its place. . . . A habit of taking the initiative, a capacity for adapting themselves to new circumstance are essential conditions of fitness in those who would direct the operations of an army corps. . . . [At present,] the highest qualities in an officer who aims at receiving a responsible post in the army are such as unfit him for assuming responsibility. He must learn to stifle his independence, to suspend his judgment, to display absolute dependence upon and blind trust in the judgment and resources of a superior officer whose mental and moral stamina he knows to be inferior to his own.

Bloch, "The Wars of the Future," *Contemporary Review*, no. 429 (September 1901), 311, 318.

and precision munitions. The demarcation between military and civilian employment may blur. Private companies, like Science Applications International Corporation or Booz Allen Hamilton, may provide target coordinates during conflicts. Hence, new public-sector activities may be required to accommodate developing technologies and network-centric operational concepts; new technical societies may have to be invented; new types of analyses may need to be developed to evaluate the interdependencies posed by C⁴ISR technologies on personnel and organizational components of combat commands; and all of the above may have to be made part of the Tactical Command joint task force organization.

Information Flows. The flow of information through an organization is impeded by several generic sources of organizational error, including imperfect and ambiguous knowledge, premature programming (a fixed commitment to a course of action taken before appropriate knowledge has been gathered), self-delusion (the tendency to act on one's preferences rather than real features of the environment), goal displacement (the substitution of short-term means for long-term ends), and uncertainty absorption (the successive editing of information as it moves up an organizational hierarchy). Organizational structures that require tight control of subordinate actions by superiors exacerbate these sources of error.

RMA transformational strategy requires attention to the development of clear cause-and-effect knowledge that relates military actions to political and military goals. The design of future military combat organizations, as well as the assignment of tasks to those combat organizations, should depend on the presence of such cause-effect knowledge. The presence of cause-effect knowledge is a prerequisite to effective operations by tightly

coupled organizations. Such knowledge helps to avoid many of
the above sources of organizational error. Those combat organizations operating under the constraints of deadlines, uncertainty, ambiguity, and imperfect knowledge, however, must
employ more features of loosely coupled organization.

Informal Organization. In both Desert Storm and Allied Force,
ad hoc and informal organizations were created or called upon
to handle critical tasks. More than those that came before, a future joint task force combat organization employing advanced
C^{4}ISR equipment will rely on ad hoc and informal organizations to mitigate performance shortfalls created by the linkages
between equipment and formal organization. This reliance on
informal organization may be the most important lesson military organizations take from the U.S. experience in Desert
Storm and Allied Force—a lesson that has important implications for staffing, peacetime training, and decision making.

   Less obvious are the consequences of overreliance on ad hoc
organizations and processes to conduct critical aspects of combat operations over long periods. People with entrepreneurial
personalities will create and work actively in these informal organizations, which may be effective in solving tactical and
short-term problems. But will the uncontrolled emergence of
informal organizations always be effective in solving long-term
problems? On aircraft carriers, informal and ad hoc organizations are drilled and exercised consciously. As personnel with
years of experience are promoted to higher positions, they teach
new generations of sailors, transmitting a sizable store of tacit
knowledge about the operation of complex technologies under
hazardous conditions. The informal organizations operating on
carriers have been able to adapt to past introductions of new
types of equipment, e.g., jet strike aircraft replacing propeller-
driven aircraft or nuclear reactors replacing fuel oil propulsion

plants. Yet, even on aircraft carriers, the past rate of introducing new technologies may be eclipsed by the rate of introducing C⁴ISR technologies. This increased pace of change raises the question: will the informal organizations respond primarily to inappropriate lessons learned long ago, forgoing the necessary experimentation to create new lessons or knowledge?

Individual and Organizational Learning

The question of how one knows one is living through a military revolution was raised in the chapter 3 discussion of rapid technological changes at the end of the nineteenth century. Those who recognize the existence of RMA-type opportunities will not necessarily have appropriate perceptions of how to achieve RMA advantages. Their description of the military-technological-organizational context, the associated explanation, and policy recommendations may also be inadequate to the situation. For example, at the end of the nineteenth century, military and political leaders recognized the potential impact of new weapons technology on warfare. Yet, they did not draw the appropriate conclusions about the mismatch between military technology and operational concepts. Nor did they have the organizational means—analytic organizations and the links among analytical and operational organizations—to identify the shortcomings to their understanding of how to conduct warfare.[13]

---

[13]There are similar examples of mismatches between the recognition of a problem and its appropriate diagnosis. For example, Douglass North noted Spain's leaders in the seventeenth century were aware of their inferior and declining competitive economic position over a period of many years. Many tracts were written analyzing the problem. But the descriptions of Spain's economic decline, the associated explanation, and policy recommendations were all inadequate. North, "Some Fundamental Puzzles in Economic History/Development," in *The Economy as an Evolving Complex System II*, eds. W. Brian Arthur, Steven N. Durlauf, and David A. Lane (Reading, MA: Addison-Wesley, 1997), 228.

There is much sloganeering about the need of the military to be flexible, adaptable, and agile, but little understanding about how to do it. Essentially, achieving flexibility, adaptability, and agility amounts to designing and operating a self-correcting organization wherein both individuals and organizations pose clear (and falsifiable) hypotheses and experiment so that they may learn from their experiences. Neither organizations nor individuals will find this an easy approach to adopt. Sometimes such an approach will mean discounting organizational or individual substantive expertise—core competencies—in solving some tasks. Individuals' and organizations' abilities to perform tasks well reinforce their attention to those tasks. People and organizations perform tasks they do well more often than they perform tasks they do less well. These frequencies of action translate into uneven experience that, in turn, translates into differences in competence. Competencies invite use, which furthers development of skills. The self-reinforcing nature of learning encourages people and organizations to become focused on those activities that they do well. Yet, as a result of learning, they may find themselves increasingly removed from other bases of experience and knowledge—and more vulnerable to environmental change. For example, the broad organization of work and labor-training institutions that worked so well for British industry in the nineteenth century became a handicap in the twentieth.[14]

It is a common canard, usually made from the vantage point of hindsight, that military organizations train and prepare only for the last war. In one respect this cliché is true. Military organizations approach new technologies, new operational concepts, and new organizations from a perspective of previous

---

[14]Richard R. Nelson, "Economic Growth via the Coevolution of Technology and Institutions," in *Evolutionary Economics and Chaos Theory*, eds. Loet Leydesdorff and Peter Van den Beselaar (New York: St. Martin's Press, 1994), 29.

experience and habits. It is reasonable to expect that experience plays a central role in deliberations about the future. Exploitation of experience gained in the last war generates clearer, earlier, and closer feedback than abstract scenarios exploring new operational concepts and new forms of organization. The evaluation of recent "lessons learned" corrects or confirms current doctrine and acquisition plans. But people (and organizations) may act on old mental models or theories of combat without ever encountering events that lead them to change their theories—including the "lessons learned" from recent combat.[15] In this respect, many of the same cognitive limits that constrain rationality in organizations also constrain human learning.[16] In a noisy environment, where one's decisions are connected with the decisions and actions of others, the simultaneous learning of many people lowers organizational performance.[17]

Two management skills are central to success in a rapidly changing and uncertain environment: the abilities to generate alternatives for operating effectively in changed environments and to implement new plans quickly.[18] These skills require an appropriate organizational context that invests heavily in experimentation. The investment in experimentation entails not only learning by doing (and thus, adding to individuals' stores of tacit knowledge) but also a research policy that permits several

---

[15]Daniel A. Levinthal and James G. March, "The Myopia of Learning," special issue, *Strategic Management Journal* 14 (Winter 1993): 102, 104, 107.

[16]Organizational intelligence is constrained by temporal myopia (learning tends to sacrifice the long run to the short run), spatial myopia (learning tends to factor effects that occur near to the learner), and failure myopia (organizational learning over-samples successes and under-samples failures). Levinthal and March, "The Myopia of Learning," 110.

[17]Richard M. Cyert and Jeffrey R. Williams, "Organizations, Decision Making, and Strategy: Overview and Comment," special issue, *Strategic Management Journal* 14 (Winter 1993): 8.

[18]See Herbert A. Simon, "Strategy and Organizational Evolution," special issue, *Strategic Management Journal* 14 (Winter 1993): 134.

separate competing strategies to be pursued simultaneously so that results may be compared.[19] Firms that conduct their own research and development are better able to use information and results from outside sources—their personnel have the intellectual capital to evaluate outside information.[20] This finding supports the development of ever more rigorous analytic and experimental organizations within the military to pose questions and evaluate experiments, games, and simulations. It should be remembered that most new ideas are bad and most innovations are unrewarding; the return from any particular social or hardware innovation is partly the experience with new ideas. Even good innovations—with hindsight—may perform poorly until experience has accumulated in using them. An organization's level of prior related knowledge is critical to its ability to recognize the value of new external information, to assimilate that information, and to apply the information to its ends. If an organization stops investing in increasing its knowledge in a rapidly developing field, it limits its ability to assimilate and exploit new information.[21]

Organizations divide attention between exploration (the pursuit of new knowledge) and exploitation (the use and development of things already known). The transformation into a twenty-first-century RMA military will require senior leaders' attention to the trade-off between the two. Applying a formula to balance exploitation and exploration is not possible,[22] but good decisions about the trade-off can be made with insight provided by the integrating experience of multiorganizational systems.

---

[19]Martin Landau and Eva Eagle, "On the Concept of Decentralization" (unpublished paper, Institute for Governmental Studies Berkeley: University of California, 1981).

[20]Wesley M. Cohen and Daniel A. Levinthal, "Absorptive Capacity: A New Perspective on Learning and Innovation," *Administrative Science Quarterly* 35 (March 1990): 129.

[21]Ibid., 136.

[22]See Levinthal and March, "The Myopia of Learning," 105.

Leaders also must recognize and analyze the trade-off between being the first to match new technologies with new operational concepts and military organizations and waiting for others to develop the capability. Being first incurs much higher research and development and experimentation costs than being a follower or imitator. However, being first may establish a capability that is hard to challenge. The decision to be an "innovating organization"—that is, to be first—is a tremendously important strategic decision. While the advantage a military derives from a particular new technology or operational concept is typically measured in years rather than in decades or generations, the advantage it may derive from an effective ability to learn how to make new things and how to do new things may be indefinite.

The Role of Path Dependence in a Transformation Strategy

Chapter 2 argued that designing a transformation strategy to move from the present to a twenty-first-century RMA organization depends on recognizing the importance of path dependence and how technology use becomes standardized. Combined with a multilevel approach, a path dependent analysis will highlight obstacles and opportunities in operating new technologies, conducting new tasks for the first time, and widely disseminating those new technologies or actions. When the number of people using a technology grows, the skills necessary to use that technology also grow, and this interaction between the numbers of people and skills makes the technology standard. For example, the pattern of weapons systems acquisition that has emerged over the last thirty years illustrates the ubiquity of the computer chip. Future military organizations and combat operations will depend heavily on computers and associated C⁴ISR equipment and software. As discussed throughout this work, this dependence on various manifestations of the computer chip will have a profound impact on the ability of personnel at all levels of an organization to carry out assigned tasks and on the effectiveness of military organizations themselves.

Analysts must understand the individual-level and organizational-level implications of technology acquisition, if they are to offer reasonable explanations for and propose remedies to unanticipated events, such as the USS *Vincennes*'s shoot-down of an Iranian airliner. Too much of the analysis of the shoot-down focused on individuals' responses to stress and too little attention was devoted to the organizational links between operating personnel and the technology—the radars, computers and cathode ray tube monitors, and software—all of which has been locked in to the force structure. Any fix to a person-machine-organization system error that only targets individuals will be ineffective because it obscures the structural context of actions and decisions.

Future Threats and Opportunity Costs. The impact of path dependence is also felt in the articulation of threats. While the probability of correctly anticipating significant features of a far-future conflict is low, existing platforms (and associated force structure and organizational structures) have long lifetimes. Consequently, most future conflicts will likely be fought with equipment and force structures being designed now that are either partially inappropriate or inadequate. Most of the tools that will be used to deal with novel future military problems will not have been designed to deal with those problems. Being alert to the role of path dependence in developing new or improved technologies and equipping the military services may help senior leaders enhance the flexibility of U.S. forces against future threats.

Challenges to Future Military Organizations

Understanding the individual- and organizational-level challenges to planning a transformation into a twenty-first-century military organization is critical when setting priorities for design. The following sections identify some of these challenges.

Trust. Relationships are more precarious in new organizations.[23] The need to establish trust is especially important among personnel operating in widely distributed locations as they learn to conduct operations according to a network-centric concept. Establishing trust among personnel who are learning to do new things underscores the wisdom of the interwar U.S. Navy aviation community, which made great efforts to create and maintain the trust of officers who were not aviators. But the need to establish trust extends beyond interpersonal relations within new organizations; it also applies to the person-machine relationship. Personnel may avoid using unstable technology or may develop ad hoc and informal fixes to a perceived weakness in the faulty technology, altering organizational capabilities in ways that may not be noticeable to senior leaders. The resulting gap between senior leaders' performance expectations and actual performance introduces another source of uncertainty into senior leaders' understanding of the combat situation.

As the four military services begin to learn network-centric operations, dedicated funds for training become an absolute necessity. The diversion of combat-ready military forces to other tasks, e.g., police actions, imposes a high opportunity cost on those troops who will conduct network-centric operations. Performing these non-network-centric operations atrophies the skills necessary to make ad hoc adjustments during combat.

---

[23]Arthur L. Stinchcombe, "Social Structure and Organizations," in *Handbook of Organizations*, ed. James G. March (Chicago: Rand McNally, 1965), 149.

The need to maintain readiness and establish trust among combat personnel learning new ways to conduct high tempo military operations may make necessary the establishment of a dedicated force—a fifth military service—for constabulary duties.

Coordination Costs. When severe constraints are imposed on the internal operation of a combat organization through nonredundant communications-sensor architectures, high coordination costs, and high information and knowledge requirements, the range of situations or missions appropriate to the organization may also be restricted. Communications-sensor systems arranged serially—largely designed and installed during peacetime—are vulnerable to single-point failure breakdowns.[24] In peacetime, a good deal of attention is devoted to the information structure of command; program managers working with limited budgets seek a sleek and efficient structure. In a stable environment, efficient communications architectures are cheap and have few coordination costs. In wartime, there is a need to pay more attention to the peculiarities of information-processing in combat organizations. The best and most resilient wartime structure for tactical operations may prize redundancy over efficiency.

Budgetary Opportunity Costs of C⁴ISR Systems. For the foreseeable future, "networked" C⁴ISR systems will be expensive. Static or declining national security budgets limit the numbers of persons who will remain in the military services. Yet, as dis-

---

[24]The Tomahawk Land Attack Missile (TLAM) planning data flow entails at least fifteen nodes—arranged serially—between national imagery and the ship launching the missile. A failure at any one of these nodes, e.g., uplink sites or an SCI router, would terminate the flow of targeting data to the launch ship. Cdr. Dan Proctor, Intelligence Officer, USS *George Washington*, in a briefing, "Carrier INTEL Support for Precision Strike," 31 October 1999.

cussed earlier, the complexity of operations using advanced C⁴ISR equipment and software will require more specialized personnel to monitor the screens, integrate and fuse information, and coordinate actions of people at all levels of the combat organizations. The services can ill afford to lose the important intellectual capital or technical skills of those who operate, maintain, and repair the complex C⁴ISR technologies. However, purchasing sufficient numbers of complex sensor-munitions systems and fielding a large enough force to wage a successful campaign imposes a high opportunity cost on the national budget, diverting funds needed for infrastructure repair, education, housing, and so on.[25] And the budgetary impact does not stop with the initial acquisition. First, advanced C⁴ISR equipment will require frequent costly upgrades, creating difficult management trade-offs among (1) the purchase of new systems and training for existing systems, (2) coordination costs in learning to operate new systems and operational costs in being proficient with existing software and equipment, and (3) complexity of the organization-equipment system and the logistics tail to ensure the equipment works in combat.

Second, the current poverty of analysis associated with the acquisition of C⁴ISR technologies increases the likelihood of poor choices. When engineers and politicians seeking to "sell" C⁴ISR systems in their political arenas fail to engage in multiple levels of analysis, they frequently underestimate the potential for costly errors due to (1) the complexity of the equipment, (2) the unexpected interactions among the types of equipment in the network, (3) the difficulty of coordinating different generations of equipment cobbled together, and (4) the failure to secure funds to ensure appropriate continual training.

---

[25]This is an argument economist Seymour Melman (and many others) made for years. See for example Melman, *Pentagon Capitalism: The Political Economy of War* (New York: McGraw-Hill, 1970).

Third, limited budgets for costly and complex new equipment will affect the ability of a nation to field force structures required by their operational concepts and doctrine. The self-reinforcing dynamic of the high cost of equipment, the uncertain technical performance of the equipment (especially in conjunction with the equipment already fielded), low procurement numbers, and the new operational concepts inappropriate to existing force structure may be exacerbated by a political dynamic to reduce funds. Insufficient funds for operational tests and evaluation of new equipment results in lower numbers of tests for that equipment and a tendency to generate favorable results from those tests conducted. A low tolerance for error of any sort manifests the incentive to generate only positive test results because a test failure likely means program cancellation. Truncated operational tests and evaluation of new systems may be inadequate, offering only insufficient and slowly accumulating knowledge about the experimental technologies. The resulting higher costs allow the procurement of fewer systems than the military organization's operational concepts require. Ultimately, the mismatch between operational concepts and procurement may impair the ability of military organizations to carry out national goals.

A Structural Reorganization

Some futurists have applied economist Joseph A. Schumpeter's observation—that each era is dominated by its own set of fundamental technologies—to military conflict. To operate effectively with those technologies that dominate a particular era, a set of compatible and supportive institutions and organizations are needed. Yet, some military organizations and organizational forms may be clearly inappropriate for a new set of technologies.

Once precision-guided munitions and advanced C⁴ISR technologies have been fully established in the U.S. force structure, other features of the nation's institutional environment become important in developing effective operational concepts and military organizations. In particular, the openness of American political institutions to the formation of multiorganizational systems increases the likelihood of smarter decision making about the acquisition of particular technologies and training for their application.

Toward what concepts of operation should military organizations evolve? How should the United States compete in specific missions? What organizational forms and arrangements may exploit U.S. technological and personnel advantages? The answer to these questions should be guided by principles developed and discussed in the previous chapters: (1) develop the ability to exploit existing knowledge and analysis in decision making, (2) conserve the attention of decision makers, and (3) limit the interdependencies among operational organizational units.[26] The application of these principles should lead to reexamination of the current command structure, which applies essentially the same organizational architecture to all conflict scenarios, and to consideration of a command structure that recognizes the impact of uncertainty, imperfect information, and ambiguity on decision making at all organizational levels. By the mid-twenty-first century, three different unified commands may be created—Long-Range Precision Strike; Constabulary (for peace-keeping and related operations), and Tactical—each organized according to the ability of military leaders to exploit cause-and-effect knowledge, to conserve their attention, and to minimize their interdependencies.

---

[26]The latter two principles are derived from Nobel laureate Herbert A. Simon. See Simon, "Applying Information Technology to Organization Design," *Public Administration Review* 33 (1973): 268–278.

A Long-Range Precision Strike Command. The features and characteristics of an organization to conduct long-range precision strike were discussed in chapter 6. Assuming the requisite cause-effect knowledge to link military actions with political and military outcomes has been developed, this command would employ the most tightly coupled structure of all military combat organizations.

A Constabulary Command. The ubiquity of global news reporting about civil wars will continue to lead to public demands for efforts to engage in peacekeeping operations. The front page of the 26 January 1999 *New York Times*, for example, showed a photograph of a young man in Sierra Leone whose hands were hacked off by rebels.[27] Such atrocities demand international action to protect noncombatants and to create the climate for effective democratic institutions to flourish. However, neither international alliances, e.g., NATO, nor the force structures of individual nations are constituted to engage in police or constabulary actions. Indeed, to the extent that national militaries are constituted to engage in police actions, they will be less well prepared to engage in increasingly technological conventional combat against other military forces. It remains, therefore, to create the organizational means to engage in police actions.

The organizational structure appropriate to the problem of peacekeeping might be similar to the notional newsroom discussed in chapter 6. That is, it would mix elements of loosely coupled and tightly coupled structure. In this way, it may cope with the political demands of senior civilians to keep apprised of the situation and to direct some actions and the military demands of combat leaders to respond quickly to developing situations.

---

[27]Norimitsu Onishi, "A Brutal War's Machetes Maim Sierra Leone," *New York Times*, 26 January 1999, A1, A6.

A Tactical Command. The Tactical Command might be the most loosely coupled of the three new commands and employ network-centric concepts most fully to engage enemy conventional military forces. As discussed in chapter 6, this type of organizational structure would best allow senior commanders to cope with uncertainty, ambiguity, and imperfect information— i.e., friction and the fog of war—under very short deadlines.

The Three Commands in the Context of Research Questions

This organization of unified commands assumes that C^2, the part of the military system that the national security community currently understands the least, may become the decisive aspect of future conflict. Understanding the nature of that conflict was the aim of the research questions posed in chapter 2. In some respects, questions 5, 6, and 7 address the same issue from different perspectives. This book has only begun to explore the far-reaching implications of these questions. Indeed, the analysis conducted here provides a better guide to the problems faced at the level of the joint task force commander than to the tactical level of military organization. Continued analysis is needed to explore the full implications of the seven questions at all levels of military organization. The following initial answers to the questions, based on the preceding discussion, offer a foundation for such further analysis.

1. How might a tactical unit, equipped with new sensor and communications equipment, operate? How might actions be coordinated with other units?

    The answer partly depends upon the task and the situation. During network-centric combat operations conducted by the Tactical Command, an informal organization might help mitigate inevitable C⁴ISR technology communication errors. The Tactical Command requires "generalists" in both officer and noncommissioned officer ranks who have been exposed to the people and problems of other specialties. Coordination among tactical units may be accomplished by interactive access to a form of intranet containing digitized terrain, feature, and location data, and information about the location and movement of friendly and enemy forces. Senior leaders also would have interactive access to such an intranet and would use it to provide guidance and support.

The senior leaders of Tactical Command and Long-Range Precision Strike Command would demarcate (and, as necessary, move) the fire-support coordination line separating deep-strike and tactical fires. In this way, senior leaders may accomplish some tasks, e.g., the long-range destruction of targets with easily identified coordinates, and then concentrate their attention on the integration and coordination of their related, but separate, efforts.

The high expense of C⁴ISR equipment, software, and associated platforms places a premium on peacetime training of tactical forces and on coordination with the Long-Range Precision Strike Command. The outbreak of hostilities may be very sudden and allow little or no slack time to learn how to fight effectively.

2. How might a theater commander operate with new sensor and communications equipment?

The Tactical Command theater commander may devote much of his time to the coordination of geographically dispersed forces. Using e-mail and video teleconferencing to coordinate forces increases the vulnerability of decision making to errors of uncertainty absorption and groupthink. Recent social psychology research on online groups and chat rooms suggests that the use of this technology may exacerbate the friction of war.[28] Online groups tend to get into more arguments and take more time to agree on a course of action than groups working face-to-face. Over time, online discussion tends to become polarized, with initially moderate individuals making extreme arguments. The online dissenter, who may have greater knowledge than the rest of the group, tends to be ignored.[29]

These initial studies of online groups and chat rooms suggest that peacetime military training in the use of intranets to conduct network-centric operations will have to (1) examine the role of "moderators" to mediate and guide online transfer of information and discussion, (2) develop new means to characterize relevant evidence, and (3) figure out how to convey doubts "off-line," to consider "intuition," and to communicate clearly in writing.

The rapidity of tactical operations (for both the Tactical Command and the Constabulary Command) necessitates that the decision process ensures situational awareness. Loose coupling of multiple agencies supplying information may help improve BDA by increasing the opportunity of those who know something about an issue to add that information to the evolving assessment.[30] Electronically connected users might query a master intranet or web-based database. Because attacks on this system might seriously degrade the ability to op-

---

[28]Patricia Wallace, *Psychology of the Internet* (Cambridge: Cambridge University Press, 1999).

[29]I am indebted to Sheryl Skifstad for the Patricia Wallace citation.

[30]This approach is similar to the "pandemonium" model of pattern recognition proposed in the late 1950s. See Oliver G. Selfridge, "Pandemonium: A Paradigm for Learning," in *Mechanisation of Thought Processes* (Teddington: National Physical Laboratory, 1959).

erate with situational awareness, redundancy of access
and service providers are required for system stability—
and if necessary, graceful degradation.

3. How might organizations and decision makers cope with
information overflow?

On one hand, organizations and decision makers
might cope with information overload simply by ignoring information that is inconsistent with plans or predis-
positions.[31] A better but more difficult solution to the
information-overload problem is to have clear ideas of
which information is important to fulfill which tasks.
This solution implies (1) the creation of extensive databases that contain relevant information and data and (2)
the development of new types of intelligent search engines or other analytic tools, such as the Google search
engine, which ranks relevant websites based on the link
structure of the Internet itself. Future intelligent search
engines might be able to display a form of base rate or
frequency data about military situations (e.g., "air superiority has been irrelevant to the conduct of a ground
campaign under the following conditions . . .") that may
be compared with the current situation facing military
leaders.

4. How should decision makers trade off tight and loose
coupling of collections of organizations? When should
decision makers emphasize one or the other?

Trade-off criteria for the use of tight and loose coupling of organizations should enhance the senior leaders'
ability (1) to provide appropriate knowledge and information to their combat leaders and (2) to focus the attention of their combat leaders on the information relevant

---

[31]This is an old problem. See R. Jeffrey Smith, "Crisis Management under Strain,"
Science 225 (31 August 1984): 907–909.

to their tasks and situation. Reliance on tight coupling (and planning) for some military tasks—assuming the causal knowledge appropriate to those tasks has been systematically gathered—should be employed whenever feasible. Tight coupling within a joint task force, for example, should be applied to targets for long-range precision strikes that are the product of groups of organizations buffered from tactical operations. However, tight coupling of operations and collections of organizations in the absence of appropriate knowledge raises the potential for operational errors, miscommunication, confusion, and organizational breakdowns.

Loose coupling within a joint task force should predominate for tactical operations that require decisions in the face of uncertainty, ambiguity, imperfect information, and deadlines. Loose coupling of combat components would allow combat leaders to query relevant C⁴ISR systems as necessary. Under these conditions, a combat leader's decisiveness and willingness to act on the information he possesses are more likely to lead to success than were he to wait to act only when he obtains complete or unambiguous information.

5. How may a large set of necessary decisions be factored and coordinated so that interactions do not impair achievement of military ends?

The answer to this question reiterates previous arguments about the need to develop appropriate cause-effect knowledge relating target sets (and the "political will" of the enemy) to political and military outcomes. For example, decisions about long-range precision strikes against strategic targets that support a regime might be partially separated from a theater commander's decisions about how to engage enemy forces. In this example, the theater commander would have full knowledge of the activities, targeting, and outcomes of the organization conducting long-range precision strikes.

Coordinating tactical operations with long-range precision strike might require intense discussion of intent (of attacks) at the senior levels. Removing long-range precision strike from the tasks conducted by the theater commander would reduce the number and complexity of tasks and problems to which senior military leaders must attend—e.g., the tactical commander would not have to deal with the "logistics" and "footprint" of forces that conduct long-range precision strikes. The advantage of this type of arrangement is that the theater commander may devote more intense attention to the information, analyses, organizations, and planning and decision making processes relevant to the tactical situation.

6. How may the complexity of senior commanders' decision problems be reduced to manageable proportions?

The complexity of senior commanders' decision problems is primarily a function of coping with imperfect information, ambiguity, and uncertainty. Existing tightly coupled organizational structures compound and exacerbate individual cognitive limits by overlaying a set of organizationally induced sources of error. The complexity of commanders' decision problems may be reduced by changing the organizational context of decisions, ie., providing commanders with organizational structures that are more appropriate to the military tasks they face. As argued in chapter 6, the problems of commanding long-range precision strikes—if appropriate causal knowledge is available—can be handled well in a tightly coupled organization. The removal of long-range precision strike from the set of tasks assigned to a commander facing enemy forces may allow him to focus on a smaller set of problems. Senior personnel in a Tactical

Command can adopt a loosely coupled organizational structure to deal with rapid changes in their own forces and in the disposition of the enemy.

7. How may a commander's attention be conserved by reducing the number of decision problems he faces?

A decision theorist will argue that to conserve a commander's attention, his decision problem must be appropriately factored. In other words, the number of interdependencies that commanders must consider must be reduced. The formation of the three new unified commands—Long-Range Precision Strike, Constabulary, and Tactical—organized differently to handle different kinds of missions should address this problem.

Implications

The above discussion reflects only the beginning of a multilevel analysis of the future of war. Yet, already this analysis has implications:

1. Peacetime training at all levels of command might require greater emphasis on developing and improving analytic ability to cope with uncertainty, imperfect information, and ambiguity under deadlines.

2. New military analytic organizations might be created to develop cause-effect knowledge necessary to employ long-range precision strikes, i.e., knowledge that relates target sets to military and political outcomes.

3. Chapters 5 and 6 included discussion of the impact on military operations of software glitches, multiple transient errors arising from equipment complexities, communications interdependencies among various sensors and processing stations, and the higher level of knowl-

edge required to use C⁴ISR equipment properly. These almost inevitable outcomes deriving from the increased digitization of existing military organizations make the organizations more vulnerable to systemic breakdowns and lower operational effectiveness. Future improvements in software and hardware stability may mitigate some of these problems. Yet, improving overall organizational robustness is made more difficult when the organizational context and an individual using the equipment are excluded from a set of possible software and hardware fixes.

Military leaders, cognizant of their forces' vulnerabilities, might be less willing to engage in conflict, while foreign governments, the State Department, and domestic lobbies might demand U.S. military intervention in international crises. This tension between military leaders and government agencies creates incentives to intervene only against very weak opponents or to declare victory and to pullout forces at the first appearance of determined and effective opposition.

4. A years-long transition period is inevitable to mesh C⁴ISR equipment with tightly coupled or loosely coupled organizational structures. In advance of firm knowledge of the complementarity of technology, organizational systems, and features of human decision making, employment of C⁴ISR equipment and associated network-centric operational concepts might result in serious operational and tactical failures. U.S. military efforts with new equipment and operational concepts might be saved only by informal and ad hoc organizations that increase the number and variety of communications and analytic links. The resulting mixture of formal and informal organizations will be too complex for a standard organization chart and will make it very difficult to isolate and diffuse lessons learned

from conflicts between organizational structures and operational outcomes.

5. Radically different products often call forth new industries, instead of being absorbed by the industries whose products they replace. For military organizations, however, introducing radically different operational concepts is more difficult because the services oppose the formation of new organizations to perform new roles and missions. The adaptability of existing military organizations to the RMA technologies, associated operational concepts, and potential new organizations might depend on whether the new RMA technologies and organizations employ the same kind of intellectual and social skills as current systems for platform-centric warfare. If the same kind of understanding is present in both modes of combat, current military organizations can likely make the switch easily. If a different skill set is necessary, the switch will be more difficult, and completely new forms of organization may be necessary. In 1998, Senator Bob Smith (R-NH) argued for new organizational forms, declaring that if the U.S. Air Force failed to devote more attention to space, a separate service might be created to do that work.[32]

For the Future

After reviewing the extensive literature on C², Col. Thomas P. Coakley noted, "the human side of C² is probably more complex and less understood than the technology side."[33] Signifi-

---

[32]Senator Bob Smith, "The Challenge of Space Power," *Airpower Journal* 13 (Spring 1999): 32–39. This article is adapted from a speech delivered in November 1998 to the Institute for Foreign Policy Analysis and the Fletcher School of Law and Diplomacy at Tufts University.

[33]Coakley, *Command and Control for War and Peace*, 180.

cant continuing research efforts should be focused on the human and organizational factors described in this book. An appropriate research program should include systematic investigation (including realistic exercises) into the relationship between organizational structures and operational capability, such as the effects of different hierarchies (relations of the center to the periphery) on operations, the dependency of the center on technology, and the organizational and technological means for "graceful" failure. Examination of such research problems would better prepare the most senior national security policy makers to reflect intelligently upon the matter of controlling twenty-first-century military forces under varying conditions.[34]

The normal interaction between problems and solutions, in which the identification of and solution to a particular problem creates new problems elsewhere, places an extremely heavy burden on the organization of wartime C^2 systems. U.S. forces must be flexible and ready to react quickly, defensively or offensively, against a competent adversary. Flexibility and the ability to act quickly assume an effective C^2 system that can perform in real or near-real time and survive enemy efforts to damage or destroy it.

Consequently, the major hazard facing senior leaders trying to balance resources devoted to exploring new concepts and technology against the exploitation of current equipment and existing doctrine is the tendency of successful leaders to adopt an option before a sufficient number of alternatives have been explored and compared. The premature adoption of a new concept or technology reduces the resources allocated to necessary exploration.

Creating a twenty-first-century RMA military requires the development of an effective organizational self-correction capa-

---

[34]Andrew W. Marshall, James J. Martin, and Henry S. Rowen, eds., *On Not Confusing Ourselves* (Boulder, CO: Westview Press, 1991), 9.

bility, which would allow the United States to be first in the intellectual task of designing organizational and operational innovations, first in ranking the effectiveness of those innovations, and first in adopting the innovations that exploit available technologies or technologies available in the next decade. And these advantages may remain indefinitely. A U.S. self-correcting organizational capability would be poorly understood but highly threatening to potential adversaries. The U.S. ability to project force effectively and gain military and political objectives would foment intense soul searching and some imitation by competing militaries. Regimes with institutional frameworks that discourage growth of knowledge, however, cannot simply adopt the technologies or the forms of successful self-correcting military organizations, as the civilian and military leaders of the People's Republic of China did discover.[35] Simple imitation of form—rather than substance—would not enhance operational effectiveness unless our adversaries were to adopt similar (i.e., democratic) institutional and organizational responses to dealing with uncertainty, ambiguity, imperfect information, and differing opinions.

---

[35]Chinese military leaders are quite interested in the RMA concept and associated technologies. Under the current institutional and organizational conditions, it may prove very difficult for China's leaders to design and implement an RMA force structure. For translations of Chinese military writing on the RMA and discussion of these writings, see Michael Pillsbury, ed., *Chinese Views of Future Warfare* (Washington, DC: NDU Press, 1996); and Michael Pillsbury, *China Debates the Future Security Environment* (Washington, DC: NDU Press, 2000).

Index

About the Author

Dr. Mark D. Mandeles formed THE J. DE BLOCH GROUP, an independent consulting company, in 1993 to examine a wide range of national security and foreign policy issues. In this capacity, he has consulted for the Director of Net Assessment, the Director of Force Transformation, the Under Secretary of Defense for Policy, Center for Naval Analyses, other Defense Department agencies and private industry. He has published essays, articles, and reviews on command and control, naval weapons acquisition, professional military education, military doctrine, nuclear strategy, military innovation, the revolution in military affairs, and ballistic missile and nuclear weapons proliferation. With Thomas C. Hone and Norman Friedman, he co-wrote *American and British Aircraft Carrier Development, 1919–1941*, published by the Naval Institute Press. With Thomas C. Hone and Sanford S. terry, he co-wrote *Managing "Command and Control" in the Persian Gulf War* published by Praeger. He also wrote *The Development of the B-52 and Jet Propulsion* published by Air University Press. Dr. Mandeles lives in Fairfax, Virginia.